OVER 50 LOOKING 30!
THE SECRETS OF STAYING YOUNG

The latest information on how to become
wrinkle resistant and fight the signs of aging.

by
Nina Anderson and Howard Peiper

Illustrated by
Richard Vail

Published by SAFE GOODS
East Canaan, Connecticut

OVER 50 LOOKING 30!
The Secrets of Staying Young

Copyright © 1996 by Nina Anderson and Howard Peiper
Illustrated by Richard Vail

All Rights Reserved

No part of this book may be reproduced in any form without the written consent of the publisher.

ISBN 1-884820-15-8-50995
Library of Congress Catalog Card Number 95-92939

1st printing April 1996
2nd printing September 1996
Printed in the United States of America

Published by Safe Goods
283 East Canaan Rd.
East Canaan, Ct. 06024
(860)-824-5301

FORWARD..

A remark often made by middle-aged and older Americans, reflects a philosophical (if erroneous) concept that converts time from a dimension (duration) as a cause of sickness and bodily degeneration, "Well, of course I have a little arthritis, I'm growing older". In this philosophy, wrinkling of the skin, graying of the hair, cataracts and other degenerative diseases are seen as the inevitable and inescapable effects of time itself.

The authors of *Over 50, Looking 30!* present authoritative, accurate information concerning vital, complicated human nutritional processes in such an interesting and informative manner. Even as a physician, especially informed and interested in human nutrition, I learned much from this book.

Each chapter has such a personal impact and meaning for the reader, that they will stop and ponder as to how the facts and knowledge gained specifically apply to them. Many chapters will be reread several times. This book is well documented and is an excellent source of reference material. Here is a book for the physician and technically trained person as well as for the layman. Non-medical people can expect technical knowledge expressed in direct yet simple understandable language, as far as food, diet and human nutrition are concerned. It will serve as a good review for even the physician and will bring the nutritionist up to date.

How I wish I could have read this book before or during my medical school education, where today students tend to get lost among the trees of technical knowledge. It is difficult for them to grasp the broader perspectives, therefore, many doctors and their patients unfortunately suffer from malnutritional disease with resultant physical and mental deterioration.   -James Balch, M.D.

INTRODUCTION...

Are you confused about the road to take for better health? Does your kitchen cabinet look like a vitamin factory and do you find that just when you settle into a new diet, you hear that science discovers that many of those foods actually harm you? Having been down that road for twenty-five years, we decided to research what the body really wants and pass this information along to you in a simple to read book, that takes a good look at what happens inside our bodies which causes the aging process to rear its wrinkled head.

We always wondered if all the vitamins we popped into our mouths, really did anything in our bodies other than work our kidneys to excrete them. If all the nutritious foods we ate were really essential, then why did we still feel tired and get colds? Why were we starting to feel old and egads! we have reached middle-age and were facing mortality. This couldn't be. We can't get old! There must be a way to reverse time.

We found some interesting ways to slow the proverbial time clock down and keep us young looking in the process. To our knowledge, no one has attempted to bring together in one book, a good look at what causes aging and write it so the non-medical person can comprehend it. You have heard that there are sixty year-olds with thirty year old minds and bodies. This proves that passing time does not mean you have to BE old. Much of it is a result of your mind set...to be old or to be young, the choice is yours.

In short, the calendar and clock, in themselves, are not toxic nor are they the origin of degenerative changes and disease. It is important that this truth be grasped, otherwise there is little point in discussing the nutritional weapons that may halt, slow down or even reverse some of the symptoms and changes that we attribute to growing old. We want to make the point, that before you load your body down with quantities of "nutrients", based on information supported by manufacturers of those products or media advertising claims, that you understand a little about how the body works. We have attempted to do your homework for you and have weeded out many details leaving the heart of the subject for you to comprehend. You can treat this material as an open door to walk through, absorb it and conduct further research using our extensive bibliography.

In treating the body as an eco-system within your skin this book gives information so you can stop polluting your personal planet, and start nourishing it. Our belief is that the mind controls our aging process. Not only can it convince you that you are young, but it can guide you to protecting your body from "terrorists" that can undermine it and cause sickness. We are not focusing on what already has been written such as vitamins, anti-oxidants, drugs, face lifts, etc. We simply provide you with a big picture so that you can plug in your pieces where they are necessary.

Our advisory staff has had success in treating and advising people for degenerative illness and the 'aging syndrome'. We value their input and have asked them to contribute their professional expertise throughout these chapters. Manufacturers of products that support our research, have included explanations of their products in our Resource Directory. Please educate yourself further by requesting supporting information from them. This book is printed in larger type for all of those people who have reached that magic age of needing reading glasses.

TABLE OF CONTENTS

PART I   GENERAL OVERVIEW...

CELLULAR BIOLOGY   1
How Your Body Works

MYTHS:
You Have To Die Of Something   9
You Are What You Eat   10
Everything In Moderation   11
The Media Never Lies   12
TRUTHS:
You're Only As Old As You Think   13
Good Health Is A Choice   14
BASICS:
Minerals Are Your Building Materials   15
Enzymes Are Construction Workers   16
Essential Fatty Acids Are The Foremen   17
Greens Keep The Termites Away   18

PART II   DETAILS...

WASTE REMOVAL   19
De-toxing as the first step to rejuvenation
MINERALS   31
Nature's last stand
ENZYMES   41
The labor force for good health
ESSENTIAL FATTY ACIDS   53
Our good guys
GREENS AND LIVE FOODS   61
The ultimate free radical fighters
GARLIC   73
A miracle cure
SKIN   83
The body's early warning system

SIGNS OF AGING   95
Balding, Hot Flashes, Arthritis, etc.
HERBS, FLOWERS, BEES AND HOMEOPATHICS   105
Supportive alternatives
THINK YOUNG   115
Visual imagery
FITNESS FOR YOUTH   123
Exercises to build bone and maintain youth

PART III   FOLLOW-UP..

RESOURCE DIRECTORY   133
Descriptions of supportive products
BIBLIOGRAPHY   144
For the reader who wants to know more

CELLULAR BIOLOGY...

To begin with, this chapter is not going to be a dry recitation of biochemistry, or a short order course in biology that will turn your hair gray, cause you to wrinkle your brow in frustration, or stress you more than you already are now. That would only serve to age you more and this book is all about looking, feeling and being younger. In this chapter I will show you, in simple lay terms, how to be young in body and spirit. If there ever was a cure for aging, it would have to exist in what you put into your body. Since food is one of the most abundant items that we put into our bodies, it would make sense to address it in some detail.

We do not want to forget entirely about the air, water and other substances that we ingest. Clean air and clean water are essential, but metabolizing these substances are simple compared to the metabolism of food. What we mean is that oxygen comes in the body through the air in the lungs no matter how dirty or how clean, provided you breath. Water is absorbed regardless of its quality, for better or worse. How the body uses oxygen via the blood is another story. The oxygen that gets into the lungs has to be transported via the blood to all the body tissues. If that blood is incapable of circulating or if it is clumped, the tissues may not get the necessary oxygen.

Food has to be digested (broken down into smaller particles), absorbed (taken from the intestines into the blood) and utilized (taken from the blood into the cells). Each of these steps is essential and if the elements ingested are missing any one of these steps, your body will not use these substances. Food is not a single entity such as oxygen or water. It consists of many different parts. These include carbohydrates (starches), protein (amino acids) and fats.

Also, the more forgotten vitamins, minerals, and most importantly.... Enzymes.

Again, each of these substances is essential. Missing only one is the difference between life and death, between youth and aging. For example, one might ingest large amounts of antioxidants yet have much damaged tissue resulting in aging, because they were deficient in the enzymes necessary to utilize the antioxidants. To make this easier to understand, let us tell you a story starting at your mouth and ending in your cells. Remember, your cells are where everything important happens. Metabolism, elimination of waste into the blood, production of all substances made by the body, energy production and utilization of all nutrients all occurs in the blood. If any ingested substance doesn't get into the cell, it doesn't get used.

So here goes the tour:
First, chewing? No not really. First, you smell or think of food. This starts your body getting ready to digest and assimilate. So you prepare some food and put it in your mouth. If that food is raw, chewing it, breaks the cell membranes of the food releasing the enzymes that start the digestion of the food. Your saliva also releases amylase to start digesting the starches in the food. If your food is cooked, chewing only breaks the cells into smaller pieces so that your stomach will have an easier time of its job. Food eaten raw does make less work for your body, in that most of the digestion is done by enzymes in the food.

If this food is cooked above 118 degrees however, those enzymes are killed and your body has to do all the digestion by itself. On another note, if you don't chew your food, the enzymes found in your saliva will not be released, preventing starch digestion. It is very important to chew our food very well, much like a cow does. Only carnivores eat quickly and chew minimally. Herbivores chew their food very well.

Next you swallow the food. It goes down into your stomach where the body secretes acids and enzymes to digest the proteins. The natural plant enzymes in the food continue to digest the proteins, fats and the starches, but enzymes made by the saliva, stop working until the food gets into the small intestine where their is less acid content than in the stomach. In the small intestine, enzymes are made by your body to digest the fats and starches. Again, if the food is raw, most of this work is done already. If it is cooked, your body has to put out a lot of energy to accomplish this task.

You may have gotten the idea by now that this is not an easy job. You are correct. It is a lot of work for your body to digest food without the help of plant enzymes. This is why we often feel tired after eating a heavy meal. And if you eat three meals a day you may feel tired after each meal. One way to avoid this tired feeling is to make sure your body has all the help it can get from plant enzymes. This does not mean you have to eat all your food raw. You can replace the enzymes found in raw food after it has been cooked by taking supplemental plant enzymes.

The small intestine is where absorption of the nutrients take place. Nutrients are substances such as proteins, carbohydrates, fats, vitamins, minerals, and enzymes. In order for your body to use these substances, they must be broken down into their smallest components. Proteins are reduced to amino acids, fats into either fatty acids, and carbohydrates into glucose. The food must also be sufficiently broken down to allow releasing of the vitamins and minerals. Food that is not broken down sufficiently suffers two fates.

One is that it may go through the intestines and feed the

"bad" bacteria and yeast's that invade your body and that should be kept to a minimum. This encourages imbalance in the bowel and may facilitate the overgrowth of bacteria and yeast, damaging the intestine and seeping into the blood where the immune system has the task of getting rid of them. Secondly, the food may be absorbed partially broken down. In the blood, products of this incompletely digested food is perceived by the immune system as a foreign invader, causing the immune system to attack them. This may lead to fatigue or the over reactivity of the immune system called allergies.

Lets not forget about the part of food that can not be digested called fiber. Food in its natural state contains all we need. Take grain for instance. The inner part of grains is the starch which we break down into glucose and use for energy. The next outer part is the germ which contains all the vitamins, enzymes, and minerals we need in order to utilize the starch. If we eat the grain without the germ, we cannot use the starch and it will build up in the body and be converted to fat. The most outer part of the grain is the hull or fiber which carries away the waste created by our bodies when we utilize the starch with the help of the germ. This is why whole grains are so important.

Consider, whether or not the food you eat contains all it is supposed to. With the onset of forced farming using chemicals, much of our food is deficient in vital substances that are needed in order to use these foods for energy. No wonder that most Americans complain of being tired. Lastly, many of our food such as corn, wheat and some fruits are hybridized. What this means is that they been weakened by genetic tampering, and the reason for the tampering is to make the food look better or taste better, not to improve its quality.

Elimination is the second most important process that the

body does. For each particle of food the body uses, it produces an equivalent amount of waste products from its use. In order to eliminate this waste we need the fiber. This brings out the importance of eating foods that contain the fiber nature put in them to help carry out the waste we would produce while using them. So eating whole foods is really all important, once you consider the nutrients and the fiber you are missing if you dare to eat white flour or other processed grain.

People often take high dosage supplements that do not contain the basic elements your body needs, to eliminate the waste that your body will produce in using these supplements. Often supplements such as these, will produce more symptoms than they will help. A good example would be taking ginseng to boost energy. Unfortunately, ginseng does not contain any fiber and if one's bowels are not functioning properly, the increased metabolism caused by the ginseng will serve to also increase the amount of waste produced by the body. This causes more poison build up by the body than without the ginseng. It is important to always consider the whole picture, and the whole person in any therapy or supplement.

On to the blood. Once the nutrients are absorbed they circulate in the blood until they get to the cells that need them, where they are then absorbed and utilized. One requirement for nutrients to get to the cells however, is proper blood circulation to the tissues. If the blood is clumped due to maldigestion, or circulation is poor due to lack of exercise, some cells may not get enough nutrients or have the ability to eliminate all of their waste leading to those cells aging more quickly.

Blood is the very essence of life. It is the medium by which all of our organs obtain nutrients as well as eliminate waste. This includes our brains, eyes, lungs, liver, kidneys, skin, hair, intestines, heart, blood vessels as well as the rest of our body tissues. It is often difficult to understand that whatever we find in the blood is found in every organ in the body. And that whatever is not found in the blood is not usually found in our bodies at all.

Another factor in utilization that is often forgotten, is a term called bio-availability. This means that a substance is useable to the body. For instance, synthetic vitamin C is not very usable to the body, and although it is absorbed into the blood, it is not easily utilized by the cells. Nutrients ingested are of no use whatsoever if we do not use them. Much of the supplements we take are simply eliminated as fast as we put them into our bodies. The reason this happens is due to the absence of trace minerals and electrolytes, which unfortunately are lacking in our food and water. Since the glacier age happened a long time ago, many of the minerals have been depleted from the soil and been processed out of our purified water.

A word of concern on altered foods. These include substances like margarine, and pasteurized, homogenized, canned, frozen, and microwaved foods. Margarine is made by a process that is quite similar to how plastic is made and only serves to damage the body. Processing foods by heating simply ensures that the enzymes in these foods are destroyed. In fact, when we eat food without enzymes, our bodies have to use its own metabolic enzymes to digest the cooked food, making the pancreatic enzyme factory work overtime. This tends to deplete stores of enzymes in other areas of the body and when the tissues level of enzymes decreases to a critical level, the cell fatigues, slows down and dies. Being that enzymes are essential to life, one can easily see how dangerous an enzyme deficiency is.

Since we started this chapter talking about aging, we feel that we ought to mention a few important reasons our cells, and therefore our bodies and minds, age. The first reason is the lack of nutrients that is paramount in the American diet. This may be due to lack of ingestion, lack of absorption or lack of utilization of the nutrients.

The second reason is a lack of elimination of the waste 'poisons' made by the body in the process of living. This lack of elimination may be due to poor bowel function, poor intestinal flora, poor circulation as well as lack of sufficient nutrients. If our cells and tissue are low in nutrients, they will not have the energy to clean out the waste. Another reason for toxicity is that the blood has to flow through the intestines in order for it to be cleansed, that is, the poisons that have gone from the tissues into the blood have to be dumped into the bowel. Stress and stimulants such as sugar and coffee stop the blood from circulation through the intestines.

All cells in the body require oxygen for their proper function. The blood, but more specifically the red blood cells are what carry the oxygen. Each red cell has to have proper amounts of iron and Vitamin B 12 (plus a multitude of other nutrients) in order to function properly. In addition to this, if the red cells are clumped together due to maldigestion or a lack of enzymes, they will be prevented from flowing easily through the capillaries which are the vessels that connect the arteries to the veins. The capillaries are the place where all of the oxygen transfer from the blood to the cells in the body occur.

Poisons in our environment known as free radicals, damage the red blood cells, changing their shape from smoothly round to an irregular shape. This change of shape decreases the surface area that normally would rub against the capillary wall causing the release of oxygen to the cells. This brings into mind the importance of antioxidants, which are substances that help to balance the bodies love/hate affair with oxygen. Oxygen, though necessary for life, can also damage body tissue if present in areas that the body does not need it. Antioxidants prevent the oxidation of cells by excess oxygen. There are many antioxidants. The best ones are not only those that get absorbed into the blood, but those that are absorbed and utilized by each individual cell in the body. Many substances are absorbed into the blood and then excreted by the kidneys or the liver. Therefore they really have no action in the cells themselves. The more "food based" these substances are, the more likely they will be used by the body.

One sign of good health is the awareness of the fact that our bodies are not in pain or discomfort. On the other hand, ill health is usually manifest by some sort of symptoms even if we happen to choose to ignore them. As you progress in reading this book you will likely see some of what I have said repeated and clarified. The concepts are not difficult, but it does take time to understand them as they are so foreign to our culture.

YOU HAVE TO DIE OF SOMETHING!

This is the most popular excuse people give for not taking care of their bodies. Smokers, drinkers, couch potatoes, sugarholics, vegetable haters, etc. all would rationalize that no matter what they did to themselves, they would eventually die....ah, but what of the quality of life while living!

YOU ARE WHAT YOU EAT!

Obviously, eating burgers will not make you a burgerhead,
but popular processed, cooked foods can definitely get a
reaction from our body. Digestive aids, laxatives, sedatives,
drugs, energy drinks are only some of the "fixes" for the
trauma we inflict on our insides because of our eating
habits, lifestyles and mental states. There is a link between
our insides and outsides. The more we "trash" our insides,
the worse we look and feel. One secret to looking young, is
to understand why we age.

EVERYTHING IN MODERATION

If this were true, we could take a wee bit of arsenic, lighter fluid and rat poison on a regular basis, with no harm. In the old days, before pesticides, pollution and processed foods, this may have been more true, but today these toxins accumulate in our bodies and accelerate the aging process and the onset of degenerative disease. Some things can be taken in moderation and even in abundance, but others should be avoided like the plague and you should learn which are which.

THE MEDIA NEVER LIES!

Advertising and media reporting can brainwash us into believing chemicals are good, drugs cannot harm, junk foods are healthy and miracle cures are available for only $19.95. It is difficult for us to judge the truth. Remember when margarine was a "heart saver"? Now we find it contains evil "trans fats". It's a war out there and you had better conduct your own research to determine what the real truth is, otherwise the yellow brick road will lead to the home for old crotchety geezers!

YOU'RE ONLY AS OLD AS YOU THINK!

The mind influences every part of your body. It chooses walking, talking, arguing, when to sleep and when to go to the bathroom. Happiness is a choice and so is good health. You can end up bent over, mindless and despondent as a retiree, or live your later years as the world's oldest competitive windsurfer. To a great extent, the choice is yours, if you take a stand and think young! Remember, be careful what you dream because you might get it.

GOOD HEALTH IS A CHOICE!

After you finish reading this book, you will have a foundation for what supports your immune system and what breaks it down. From that point on, you can choose to nurture or pollute your "personal planet". Healthy choices will not keep birthdays away, but they will make your former classmates wonder who the young chick is at their reunion. If you choose to keep your head in the sand, you may find yourself falling over the edge into wrinkle canyon.

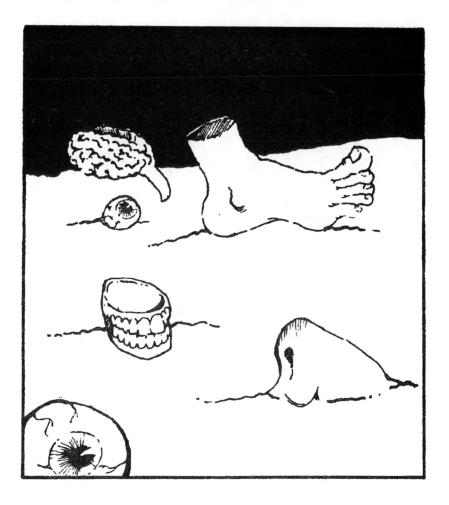

MINERALS ARE YOUR BUILDING MATERIALS!

In order to build a healthy, youthful body, you must start with strong, efficient parts. Minerals, with electrolytes, are essential to the make-up of body parts and without these trace elements, the structure will not hold together very well. Over time, mineral deficiencies will cause the walls to groan, the siding will show cracks and blemishes, parts of the structure will sag and the roof might lose its shingles. Premature aging will be inevitable.

ENZYMES ARE CONSTRUCTION WORKERS!

Not much happens in the body without enzymes. Not only do they digest food, but they fight disease and regulate almost every function that supports life. Anytime you put cooked or processed food into your body these construction workers must stop building the body, and run over to digest the food. Raw foods carry their own enzymes so don't need to pull in the troops for help. When enzymes are diverted from their body building function, father time can do his dastardly deed of premature aging.

ESSENTIAL FATTY ACIDS ARE THE FOREMEN!

Construction workers must follow blueprints in order for the structure to go together properly. The foremen direct the operation and send messages that help get the job done properly. Without the essential fatty acids, the enzymes don't get proper messages and may in effect, do the wrong thing which contributes to the aging process. They must also be balanced, as one loud mouthed foreman can do more to upset the harmony of the workers, than two complementary ones working for a common goal.

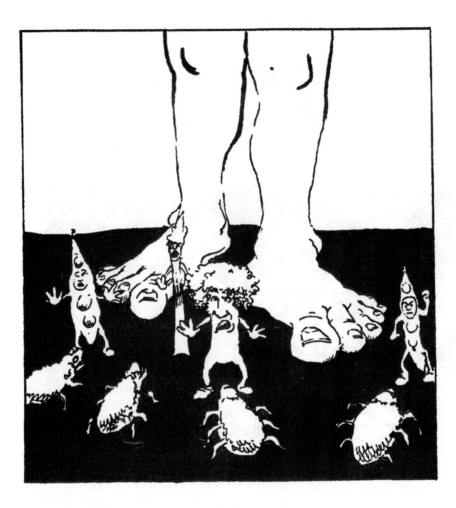

GREENS KEEP THE TERMITES AWAY!

Disease, vermin, bugs, parasites, toxins can all whittle away at the body and cause its eventual demise. Fortifying the structure against these attackers is the key role of the immune system which itself must be fortified by nutrients we supply. Micronutrients, kelp, Chlorella, wheatgrass, barley grass, veggies, Chlorophyll and other antioxidants can keep the body's "dukes up" to defend itself against any toxic onslaught. Without these, we offer a happy home to chronic illness, senility and old, old skin.

WASTE REMOVAL..

Key factors in promoting aging and degeneration are directly related to our lifestyles and habits. When we are born our internal organs are absolutely clean and hopefully devoid of toxins. If we could preserve this pristine state, we would have baby soft skin throughout our lives and may delay degenerative disease. Unfortunately from the moment of birth, we are subjected to unfriendly bacteria, parasites and foreign toxins that all tax our immune system to the ultimate. If we could only think of our bodies as an eco-system in itself, we would be more diligent in avoiding pollution and maintaining that critical balance as nature intended.

Many of us take better care of our cars than of our bodies. We know that if we put water in our gas tank, our engine won't run. It's the same as if we put a poison in our body. But if we only put a little water in the gas, our engine would still run, but not very well. This is what we are doing to our bodies with air and water pollution, toxic chemicals and our over processed, additive laden foods. Since we cannot avoid many pollutants and do make the choice to eat foods that we crave, even though we know they shock the body, it is necessary to establish regular programs to remove this debris from our "personal planet".

To begin with, we must first understand the mechanics of our engine. Our total digestive tract (from mouth to anus) is approximately 32 feet long. When we consume highly processed foods, this tubing becomes dangerously encrusted over the years. When our digestive system has this barrier built up inside, it prevents nutrients from getting absorbed into the blood stream. The body needs its "food" and if it is unable to access these nutrients, the organs will receive less than perfect "fuel" and therefore not function properly.

The main anti-aging organs are the glands which produce hormones and the organs which de-toxify the body. Scientists believe that if hormones dwindle or lose their potency, the body will age. George Fahy of the Jerome Holland Laboratory of the American Red Cross in Rockville, Maryland, has said that research has shown if missing hormones are replaced, aging can be reversed. Since the glands that secrete these hormones are dependent on proper nutrition from the body, common sense would indicate that a starved gland would not work properly.

ENDOCRINE SYSTEM

PINEAL: Cone shaped gland at the base of the brain that secretes melatonin which helps synchronize biorhythms and is the "sleep" hormone.

PITUITARY: The body's "master gland" that stimulates the adrenals, thyroid, pigmentation-producing skin cells and gonads.

THYROID: Metabolism stimulating gland that controls body heat production and bone growth.

PARATHYROID: A gland that regulates the use and function of calcium and phosphorus in the body.

THYMUS: Locate behind the breastbone, this gland is important in the development of cell-mediated immune responses.

ADRENALS: Crucial to controlling metabolism, this gland also produces hormones that maintains blood pressure and the body's salt and potassium balance.

PANCREAS: An abdominal organ that secretes insulin and glucagon to control the utilization of sugar, the body's energy source.

OVARIES: Female glands that produce estrogen and progesterone.

TESTES: Male glands that secrete testosterone to stimulate sperm production and development of male characteristics.

When glands do not work properly, they promote degenerative disease and a breakdown of the entire body's eco-system that is interdependent. The body is also dependent on a proper acid/alkaline balance, know as pH. Acids are chemical compounds that have the ability to supply positively charged hydrogen ions to a chemical reaction. Akalies are chemical compounds, called bases, that have properties opposite to acids and tend to neutralize them, forming salts.

There is no ideal neutral state for acid/alkaline balance as the intake of food and water constantly changes this balance. An acidic body fosters the condition for disease to get a foothold. This imbalance can be created by eating too many acid forming foods and can also be caused by conditions of the body, such as vomiting, diarrhea, Diabetes or from some kidney diseases. It is extremely important when undertaking any detoxification program to monitor your pH and maintain a slightly alkaline condition (urine pH above 6.4). Some foods that promote alkalinity are vegetables, sprouts, potatoes, cereal grasses and most fruits. Sugars, meat, dairy, alcohol and most grains are acid.

As toxins are fought off within our bodies, the eliminatory organs bear the responsibility of removing these foreign invaders. Flushing them out not only requires these organs to be in top physical condition, but it also demands lots of water. When man created alternatives to water (soda, coffee, booze), it set the stage for constipation. Many liquids are actually dehydrators and therefore it is absolutely necessary to drink at least eight glasses of water daily or even more if you are removing poisons from your body.

Drinking water can be a risk in itself as many sources are polluted, chlorinated, fluoridated and bacteria infested.

Purified or bottled water are required for any detox program because we don't want to add more toxins during our cleansing program. Although our eliminatory organs can use lots of water to help them with their job, we also must be careful to replace lost electrolytes (minerals) that are a casualty of the flushing see chapter, *Minerals*. If you have prepared your body properly by creating a slightly alkaline pH and consuming a good bit of water on a regular basis, you can consider detoxing through different methods.

Blood cleansing can be assisted by going on a 3 to 7 day juice fast (organic). If you think you are really toxic, fast for only 3 days at one time because more aggressive programs may quickly release too many poisons creating an overload in the bloodstream. If you suspect you have heavy metal poisoning beware of quick detox programs for the same reason. Aged Garlic Extract can be added to your diet as an alternative, because it is a chelator of heavy metals.

Some herbs that can be used to detoxifiy the blood are Red Clover, Hawthorn, Alfalfa, Nettles, Sage, Horsetail herb (silica), Echinacea, Licorice, Garlic, Milk thistle, Pau d'arco, Gotu kola, Lemon grass and Yerba santa. These herbs will also supply you with concentrated amounts of chlorophyll, helping to alkalize your pH. Detoxing may cause some symptoms such as headaches, nausea, bad breath, and body odor as the cleansing process progresses. Vitamin C is useful at this time to help keep the body alkaline, encourage oxygen uptake and promote creation of new tissue.

The liver, kidneys and the lymph glands are targets for disease because as eliminatory organs, they see their share of toxins, some of which take up lodging and remain for long periods of time. Flushing them out possibly may prevent them from growing into cancer, immune suppressants, etc. The liver is the body's most complex organ that converts everything we eat, breathe and absorb through the skin into life-sustaining substances. It is a highly condensed circulatory organ and produces natural antihistamines, manufactures bile to digest fats, excretes cholesterol, aids digestion and prevents constipation. It metabolizes proteins and carbohydrates, is a storehouse for vitamins and minerals and also secretes hormones and enzymes. We abuse it constantly, but it has the amazing ability to continue to function when 80% of its cells are damaged.

If you feel any of the following symptoms on a chronic basis, you may be in need of a liver cleanse: dizziness, dry mouth, slow elimination, mental confusion, unexplained weight gain, depression, major fatigue, PMS, constipation and food or chemical sensitivity. Since the skin is the body's largest organ, a liver cleanse might start there. Using an enzyme body wrap which includes, Alfalfa, Ginger, Dandelion root, Spearmint, Capsicum, Cinnamon. Bladderwrack, in a base of Lecithin, vegetable glycerin, aloe, olive oil, grapeseed oil and beeswax may also give great benefits to the skin. *excerpted from Detoxification & Body Cleansing by Linda Rector-Page, ND, PhD.

A liver flush tea could also be beneficial taking 2-3 cups daily for one week. The tea could contain the herbs, Milk thistle seed extract, Dandelion root, Watercress, Yellow dock root., Pau d'arco, Hyssop, Parsley leaf, Oregon grape root, Red sage, Licorice, and Hibiscus flower. As with all cleansing programs, you must maintain a slightly akaline diet. As you rebuilt the liver, you should avoid dairy, alcohol and caffeine. The addition of royal jelly, Chlorella and cereal grasses, and the anti-oxidants Vitamin A, C and E will help to restore the liver's strength. Raw liver extract (from clean sources) combined with aged garlic extract, vitamins B1 and B12 become an excellent rebuilding tonic.

Detoxifying the liver and the blood cannot be accomplished effectively without also cleaning the digestive tract. If the body is constantly being poisoned from one source, the effects of a cleaner liver and blood will be short lived. People suffer from malnutrition and auto-intoxication because of a gradual build up of many layers of mucoid plaque substance in the intestinal tract. Just like hard water builds scale on the inside of your pipes, so does your toxic eating habit affect the intestines.

When this plaque is present, there may be serious interference with the digestive process. Not only could constipation be a factor, but bigger than that, malnutrition. Any vitamins or healthful foods that we put in our bodies would be wasted money, as much of their nutritive elements would just pass through. Inside this encrusted wall lies the beginning of diverticulitis, colitis, colon cancer and a host of other diseases. The putrefied and stagnant pockets of poisons and harmful bacteria can fester and cause seepage into the bloodstream where these toxins travel to weaker parts of the body, break down the immune system and cause debilitating illness. Unfortunately symptoms resulting from toxic overload in the digestive tract are misdiagnosed, and the treatment may not be effective until the cause is eliminated (cleansing the bowel).

Something that no human ever wants to admit to, is that they may have worms. Medical textbooks have revealed that over 55 million American children have worms, and the kids may come from clean environments. People get infected from flies, mites, food, pets, fingers, feces and from the air. Their ideal environment is the digestive tract and they protect themselves from de-worming measures by hiding in the impacted layers of plaque. Over 134 kinds of parasites can live in the human body, with the World Health Organization naming parasitic diseases as among

24

the six most harmful infective diseases in humans.

Parasites can cause many symptoms from digestive disturbances such as loss of sleep, headaches, anemia coughing, blindness, skin ulcers and muscle pain, etc. Roundworms lay over 200,000 eggs per day and hookworms lay 5-10,000 eggs a day and can live for fourteen years. Once they are in your body, in addition to possible use of new drugs, a way to remove them is to clean your digestive tract and leave these parasites homeless.

There are many ways to cleanse the colon including enemas and colonics (giant enemas that go "way up"). A more pleasurable way to foster this complete elimination of the digestive tract, is through herbal and oral ingestion method. Liquid bentonite and psyllium are key ingredients in moving plaque out of the system. Bentonite is a clay that acts like a sponge absorbing toxic debris from the alimentary tract. It can absorb 180 times its own weight. It should be used with psyllium husk powder which facilitates the bentonites removal, along with the parasites and toxins. Obviously, lots of water should be taken with these substances to facilitate easy removal. It is not uncommon for people to eliminate 20, 30 or 50 feet of waste from their intestines during this type of cleanse. (I wonder how they went about measuring this!)

Along with these substances, the following herbs should be used for the reasons described:

Plantain breaks up intestinal mucoid substance. It is also good for the liver and kidney.

Barberry Bark is a powerful stomach and intestinal cleaner and blood purifier.

Myrrh helps build the immune system and helps rebuild the digestive system and remove gas.

Rhubarb Root act as a tonic to the liver and gall ducts. It helps cleanse the mucous membranes in the digestive system and is an excellent liver cleanser.

Fennel seed helps remove waste from all parts of the body, kills pinworms and calms the nervous system during the cleanse.

Ginger root removes some of the symptoms associated with the detoxifying process including headaches and an unsettled stomach. It also improves the effect of the other herbs used in the process.

Cascara Sagrada bark keeps things moving and rebuilds the peristaltic action in the intestines. It increases the secretions of the stomach, liver and pancreas thereby stimulating the removal of the mucoid substance.

Golden Seal stops infections and eliminates poisons.

Capsicum increases the effectiveness of the other herbs, and assists in the cleansing and rebuilding of the digestive system.

Red Raspberry Leaf helps prevent hemorrhages and diarrhea and creates an astringent and contracting activity within the intestinal membranes that helps dislodge mucoid crust.

Lobelia removes congestion and other obstructions from the body and helps with the elimination channels, especially the lymph.

*herbal descriptions excerpted from Cleanse & Purify Thyself by Dr. Richard Anderson, ND, NMD

There are many other colon cleanse methods that use olive oil, lemon juice, apple juice, Epsom salts, etc. We hesitate advising you to use any of these treatments unless you are under the care of a naturopathic or allopathic physician, because your body chemistry is finely tuned and any major change, although for the better in the end, could have hazardous side effects. One of the side effects of detoxifying is emotional instability. When toxins are released they may have "memories" attached to them that have been stored in the cells, thus emotions such as grief, anger and fear may be manifested. Be aware of this and identify it as part of the cleansing process and not a mental problem.

Once you have detoxified, it is very important to rebuild the good bacteria in the intestinal tract and to take foods and supplements that support the immune system. All this will benefit the anti-aging process. In the following chapters we cover nutritional aspects that support good health and we suggest that you familiarize yourself with this material in order to make an educated decision about your own body. In the rest of this chapter, we will discuss the need for proper balance of intestinal flora.

The composition of friendly bacteria living in the intestines varies. There are over 100 trillion viable bacteria living together in symbiotic or antagonistic relationships inside the digestive system. They possess diverse enzymes that perform varied types of metabolism converting substances into compounds that can affect nutrition, physiologic function, drug efficacy, carcinogenesis, resistance to infection and aging. The intestinal flora can be upset (more bad guys that good guys) because of antibiotics, stress, influenza, excessive intake of alcohol and acid forming foods, exposure to disease and as part of the aging process.

When this upset occurs our ability to process nutrients diminishes, we feel bloated, are constipated and develop a "leaky gut". Lack-luster eyes, poor skin, dull hair and excessive wrinkles are all subtle signs that one's intestinal flora need friendly bacteria. In a healthy human being, Acidophilus bacteria exist from the upper part of the small intestine to the lower part of the small intestine and Bifidobacterium exist from the lower part of the small intestine to the large intestine. These lactic acid bacteria decrease the pH in the intestines (more acid) thereby producing substances which suppress harmful bacteria. They also activate macrophages (toxin eaters) which also suppress the harmful bacteria. The large intestine is the main battle ground for the conflict against the bad bacteria.

In the small intestine, Acidopilus is the main warrior whereas in the large intestine, large amounts of

Bifidobacterium exist. In order for it to get to the large intestine, the bacteria must travel through the stomach acids, which may do it in. (Anytime you take supplements of "friendly bacteria" do so at the end of a meal because they can sneak through when bacteria acid has been diminished from food processing.) It was long thought that the Lactobacillus bulgaricus lactic acid bacteria in yogurt was the answer. Studies have reported that this bacteria is unable to reach the intestines alive and therefore has been replaced by L.acidophilus and Bifidobacterium which seem to endure stomach acids better, especially if supplemental forms are taken with food (temporarily decreases the acidity in the stomach long enough for the good bacteria to pass through). B.longum, L.acidophilus and B.bifidum are three species of the most prevalent bacteria and are very compatible with one another. If these cultures are the result of human isolates, such as found in Kyo-Dophilus®, they will be extremely bioavailable in the body.

Important roles played by these tiny bacteria, especially Lactobacillus Acidophilus include production of digestive enzymes, protecting the surfaces of intestinal mucous membranes, suppression of undesirable bacteria, reduction in gas and bad breath, production of many of the B vitamins and suppression of intestinal disorders. Lactobacillus also is undergoing research regarding its usage in cancer therapy.

In addition to taking the good intestinal bacteria, some cultivated herbal yeast supplements can help the body defend against the "bad guys". Since these yeast cells are rich in optimum combinations of many essential substances such as protein, carbohydrates, minerals, trace elements, amino acids, vitamins and enzymes, they can be extremely helpful in restoring the strength to the beneficial bacteria.

In an interesting experiment conducted in 1977 by the

Biochemical Laboratory of the Swiss College of Technology in Zurich, whereby human cells (in vitro) were cultivated under hypo- and hyper-gravity conditions in the NASA space shuttle. Weightlessness in astronauts has been shown to inhibit the production of the lymphocytes necessary for the body's defense system. When a yeast supplement, BIO-STRATH, was introduced, the result showed that the activity of the cells, which is partially lost under microgravity, could be offset or compensated to a considerable extent. Other studies revealed that this substance has also been shown to have good infection fighting ability, especially in older animals. Cereal grass and garlic are also welcome additions to the body after a cleansing and they are discussed in their own chapters.

The information presented here is meant to be taken as the first step to regaining youth. If we relate back to the automobile analogy, we need to change our oil. It has become clogged and will effect our engine performance. Once the old contaminated oil has been removed (toxins), we can add new (bacteria) and give ourselves a better chance of preventing illness and pushing back the effects of time.

Recommended reading:

Achieve Maximum Health, Colon Flora, The Missing Link in Immunity, Health & Longevity by David Webster; Hygeia Publishing

Cleanse & Purify Thyself by Dr. Richard Anderson, N.D, N.M.D

MINERALS...

If you want to live to be 100 and still have vitality and physical prowess, then this chapter is for you. Scientific research shows that the Hunzas, a 2000 year old civilization in the Himalayas, live far beyond the age of the average American. The Hunza quality of life far surpasses ours, the experience little or no disease and age with increased mental alertness, sexual appetite and more! What appears to be the chief reason for good health, is attributed to their mineral-rich waters and especially their content of the very minerals that are dangerously low in most commercial and public waters.

The Hunza's drink mineral rich water from mountain sources flowing underground and on the surface, down streams lined with rocks, which release not only calcium, but all other minerals and *trace-elements*. Electrically charged, positively or negatively, from the friction of flowing and tumbling over rocks, this water provides useable minerals. Those people advocating demineralized or purified water, like to emphasize that even if the minerals were useful, drinking water constitutes only a minor contribution to our daily intake of essential minerals and trace elements. They state that food sources contain all our mineral needs and therefore, minerals from drinking water are insignificant.

Obtaining minerals from vegetable sources is becoming more difficult each year, as the mineral content of our soils has decreased dramatically, with topsoil (the nutrient-rich ground cover) measurements declining from 3 feet two hundred years ago, to less than 6 inches today. The decline is due partly to erosion and largely to faulty agricultural techniques such as over grazing and the lack of crop rotation. Acid rain can also contribute by lowering the pH of the soil, causing many of the remaining minerals to become locked up and unavailable to plants, which now substitute by taking up toxic pesticides, fertilizers and inorganic aluminum (from the acid rain).

Food processing further depletes our food supply. Among the nutrients missing from and/or refined out of our food supply, are the vitally important "trace minerals". These are needed in very small amounts by the body and include such minerals as organic copper, zinc chromium, selenium, and iodine. These and other trace minerals plus certain macro minerals (those needed in large amounts) form the electrolytes which provide the body with vital electrical energy needed to carry out all functions.

The maintenance and/or restoration of balance is a key to health. Basically we are healthy to the degree at which the body is able to maintain homeostasis, a steady state resulting from electrolyte balance. Electrolytes are minerals salts which are capable of conducting electricity when placed in a solution. In the body, the bloodstream provides the fluid medium, while the minerals are supplied from food and water, and in some instances nutritional supplements.

In the face of today's mineral deficiencies, the body's homeostatic capabilities have broken down. The resulting energy loss and imbalance have led to impairment of bodily functions and the development of disease. To restore homeostasis, the electrolyte minerals must be provided to the body in the proper form, combination and amount. The balance of minerals (mineral homeostasis) is as important a consideration in health, as their availability and assimilation. Minerals can compete with one another for absorption, especially if too much of one is available, and not enough of others. For example, too much zinc can unbalance copper and iron levels in the body and large amounts of calcium (2000 mg.) reduce absorption of magnesium, zinc, phosphorus and manganese.

A similar unbalancing of minerals can occur with excessive intake of single vitamins, either by producing a deficiency or increasing the retention of a particular mineral. A high intake of vitamin C decreases copper's absorption and will contribute to a deficiency. Stress, aging, illness, athletic training and taking medicines all increase normal electrolyte requirements. Drugs may deplete minerals, by increasing their excretion or interfering with mineral imbalance. For example, antacids, laxatives, anti-convulsants, steroids, over consumption of protein and antibacterial agents are known to produce a deficiency of calcium and vitamin D. They exert a chelating action upon the calcium and antagonize the metabolic effects of vitamin D.

Minerals play an integral role in the health of the immune system. Antibiotics will affect their absorption. This includes zinc, which is important in the production and health of our T-cells. Thus, it makes sense why the lack of zinc and the reduction of healthy intestinal (friendly) bacteria, leads to a weakening of the immune system and increased vulnerability to opportunistic infections and yeast infections like Candida.

We are vibrating beings. The stronger the inner vibration, the healthier we are. The amplitude of body electricity alters in exact proportion to the amount of alkaline and acid-forming chemicals internally present at any one moment. Whether a substance is alkaline or acid is determined by its pH. The alkaline cells are tiny bundles of enzymes that produce energy and work within a very specific pH margin. The enzymes that work within the cell can only function when the fluid is as close to neutral pH as possible (except in the stomach which is very acid). Anything that changes the pH of the cell environment can inactivate or change the level of activity of the cellular enzymes possibly resulting in cellular starvation and cellular death.

A urine pH of 6.2 is best for human body function. However, it is impractical for the average person to constantly check their urine throughout the work day. So, we have included a chart on the next page, that states what foods are acid forming and what foods are alkaline forming. By using the chart, you can even determine with a reasonable degree of certainty your alkaline-acid levels over an extended period of time.

With the average American very high in acid foods, we must protect the balances of the body's various systems with minerals, some of which are acid forming such as chlorine, sulphur and phosphorous and others, alkaline like calcium, sodium, potassium and magnesium. Since we are assaulting the body with high levels of acid foods, we must balance it with alkaline minerals. Since metabolic waste is in the form of some type of acid, the body often unites some of the base minerals with these waste acids and eliminates them through the urine. Very rarely is alkalinity a problem, although overdose of the over-the-counter alkalizers has been known to produce this condition.

Acid/Akaline Forming Foods

Fruits:
Acid: Cranberries, Strawberries, Sour fruits
Akaline: Apples, Bananas, Citrus fruits, Grapes, Cherries, Peaches, Pears, Plums, Papaya, Pineapple, Berries, Apricots, Olives, Coconut, Dates

Vegetables:
All vegetables are alkaline including potatoes, squash and parsnips

Grains:
Acid: Brown Rice, Barley, Wheat, Oats, Rye
Alkaline: Millet, Buckwheat, Corn, Sprouted grains

Meat/Dairy:
All meats and dairy products are acid except non-fat milk

Nuts/Seeds:
Acid: Cashews, Walnuts, Filberts, Peanuts, Pecans, Macadamia, Pumpkin, Sesame, Sunflower, Flax
Alkaline: Almonds, Brazil nuts, All sprouted seeds

Beans/Peas:
Acid: Lentils, Navy, Aduki, Kidney
Alkaline: Soybeans, Limas, Sprouted beans

Sugars:
All sugars are acid except honey

Oils:
Acid: Nut oils, Butter, Cream
Alkaline: Olive, Soy, Sesame, Sunflower, Corn, Safflower, Margarine

It is our opinion, acid wastes literally attack the joints, tissues, muscles, organs, and glands causing minor to major dysfunction. If they attack the joints, you might develop arthritis. If they attack the muscles, you could end up with myofibrosis (aching muscles). If they attack the organs and glands, a myriad of illnesses could occur. The more acidic we are, the lower our immune system becomes. The more protein (meat) we ingest, the more acidic our bodies become and therefore our immune system becomes weaker. Adding sugar to our systems enables the body to become even weaker. Alkaline-forming substances create powerful and sustaining results which lead to superior health. The more extreme the deviations in pH, the more extreme the health symptoms one can experience. The goal in a day's time is to end up pH balanced but slightly more on the alkaline side than on the acid.

We hear a lot today about benefits of "oxidative" therapies. These therapies utilize such substances as hydrogen peroxide and ozone which have the effect of increasing the amount of oxygen at the cellular level. Without adequate oxygen in our tissues, metabolism is adversely effected, as is the body's ability to eliminate toxins. Lack of oxygen in our bodies is reflective of a lack of oxygen in the body of the earth. Two hundred years ago our air was composed of 38 percent oxygen, 1 percent carbon dioxide. Today, it is 19 percent oxygen and 25 percent carbon dioxide. This increase in carbon dioxide and the decline of oxygen in our environment is largely a result of pollution and deforestation of our soils.

While the oxidative therapies are successful in terms of supplying the body with much needed oxygen, they supply that oxygen from the outside, doing nothing to improve the body's own oxidative ability. When vitamins, minerals and enzymes are supplied, we have the same situation. The body benefits as long as the substance is supplied, but nothing has been done to enable it to increase its own production of free radical scavengers. The key to enhancing the body's ability to produce enzymes is the same key that normalizes all vital functions, and that is the restoration of homeostasis (electrolyte balance). Electrolytes are formed when certain minerals come together in solution and create electrical activity, providing energy for the body. Water cascading down a rocky stream creates electrolytes.

Enzyme production in the body is dependent upon minerals which are the catalysts that make enzyme function possible. The key to oxygenating the body doesn't lie in providing extra oxygen from the outside, nor is it only in improving the body's ability to produce anti-oxidants enzymes by providing them from an outside source (though these could be a temporary help). In both cases it lies in restoring electrolyte balance. Electrolytes are the nature's own oxygenators and they provide the energy necessary for us to produce the anti-oxidant enzymes needed to destroy free-radicals, the by-products of oxidation. As we mention in the skin care chapter, electrolytes also enhance tissue oxygenation and aid in the reduction of free radical formation. The net result... electrolytes can be a major factor of slowing down our skins aging process.

Where do we find these electrolytes? Nature gives us water that flows and swirls over rocks, picking up the minerals and creating vortexes which produce an electrical charge. This action of water causes the inorganic minerals, to undergo a transmutation process, changing form from colloidal to crystalloid. A crystalloid is a substance, like a crystal, which forms a true solution and can pass through a living membrane. Crystalloid minerals when they are electrically charged and found in solution, contain electrolytes. This form of mineral is assimilated 100 percent by the body and when other nutritional supplements are taken along with trace minerals (electrolytes) they become 100 percent bio-available (absorbed in the body where they are needed). Colloidal minerals from soil and rock, are inorganic, and were designed by nature to nourish plants which convert these minerals into an organic usable form for us. Food source minerals are not, totally absorbed by the body and therefore, make liquid crystalloid mineral supplements a better choice.

Serious age-related disorders like senility, are linked in several ways to electrolyte imbalance. Trace minerals are involved in the function of the minor blood vessels and capillaries in the brain, as well as the absorption of amino acids (protein) which the brain needs. The more efficient the circulation and transportation of oxygen the better the memory remains in tact over the years.

It is known that the brains of Alzheimer's patients contain abnormally high levels of aluminum. Aluminum has an enzyme inhibitory potential and aluminum deposits prevent the brain from using vitamin B12. A lack of B12 allows the nerves to become hard. Some Alzheimer's patients also become very aggressive which may give a further clue to aluminum/Alzheimer question. A study was done on aggressive boys in a detention home. Every one tested had abnormally high aluminum levels. Sufficient intake of zinc, calcium and magnesium can stop aluminum from accumulating in the brain. Our bodies react a little like the plants and need a balance of minerals, otherwise excessive levels of toxic minerals can be taken up by the cells and tissue. In recent studies it was found that many mineral supplements contained inorganic aluminum. It would be prudent to query the manufacturer and take only those that could assure you of being aluminum-free.

Mineral balance is critical, especially for the athlete. If

copper is in short supply, iron utilization will decline and produce symptoms like fatigue and lack of stamina. In addition, the high volume oxygen intake during athletic exertion oxidizes blood cells faster than normal and increases the chance of anemia. A high intake of meat and other proteins leads to an increase in the metabolic rate, part of which is achieved due to calcium and magnesium excretion. Loss of both these minerals can result in cramping, spasms, and irregular heart beat. Iron deficiency interferes with the formation of special enzymes in the body that affect muscle functions.

Zinc is another trace mineral that is lost during a workout, and could contribute to a male dysfunction. This mineral is used by the body for the production of a normal level of healthy sperm. In men with a low sperm count the replacement of lost electrolytes including zinc, brings their levels back to normal in a relatively short time (if there is nothing else causing the disorder). Impotence can also be associated with mineral deficiencies. It is thought that a significant number of men with this problem have atherosclerosis of the penile arteries, caused by a diet too high in certain fats and sugar, but most importantly, too low in trace minerals including chromium and manganese. Narrowed blood vessels restrict blood flow and limit erection. Chromium and manganese enable body systems to digest and excrete fats before they can become deposited on artery walls. Chromium also regulates mood swings, regulates blood sugar and blocks fat uptake. Trace minerals in liquid electrolyte form also keep minerals in balance so they won't become part of the arterial plaque.

Female athletes are especially prone to mild anemia or iron deficiency. Iron depletion is common and often goes undetected. Excessive physical activity often leads to loss of menstruation which stems from the body's depletion of minerals and its attempt to hang on to those which remain. Athletes may become deficient in many minerals, especially if the diet consists of refined foods and electrolytes are not replaced after workouts.

For any athlete or body builder, trace minerals or electrolytes need to be the first nutritional consideration. They work in the body to produce good assimilation and metabolism of nutrients and the breakdown of proteins into amino acids. Minerals get involved in the building of new tissue, keep joints, bones, tendons and ligaments strong and flexible, help to keep the entire cardiovascular system healthy, quench damaging free radicals and maintain the strength of the cells and their fluid levels. Everything taken into the body needs trace minerals to make it work.

Minerals add back the life force to water. Tachyonization™ re-aligns water at a sub-molecular level, increasing the bio-energetic potential of the water. Using the accomplishments of scientists like Nikola Tesla and Henry Moray, the molecular structure of natural materials like silica, water, oil, cotton and silk can now be re-aligned, transforming them into antennae which attract life force energy. Drops of this water taken sublingually breaks the blood-brain barrier and instantly provides balancing life force energy to the body, increases the ability to focus and heightens the sense of well being. Taken along with added minerals, you have one of the secrets to longevity.

Recommended reading:

Electrolytes The Spark of Life, Gillian Martlew,N.D., by Nature's Publishing Ltd.

ENZYMES...

It has been suggested by many scientists that people get old before their time because of enzyme exhaustion and that people are old at 40 because of the lack of enzymes, while others are young at 80 because of the abundance of enzymes. As we age our body's enzymes decrease in number and activity level if we don't add supplements. Without a good supply of enzymes, antioxidants have a more difficult time of fighting wrinkles, a key sign of aging. Without enough enzymes the body is unable to detoxify properly, reflecting this poisonous condition in our skin.

Stomach acid is essential for efficient nutrient absorption and as people age, they lose the ability to secrete the necessary levels of hydrochloric acid required for proper digestion. At forty, people secrete only sixty-five percent of the normal levels of digestive enzymes, and at sixty-five it reduces to fifteen percent. Looking young depends on being young inside your body and adding an abundance of enzymes will head you in that direction.

The male sperm is equipped with a minute amount of enzyme to dissolve a tiny crevice in the egg membrane, therefore, from the instant of conception enzymes play an important part in all life processes. It is thought that diabetes and leukemia may be due in part to missing or faulty enzymes. Medical researchers are using enzyme therapy to reduce blood clots, as an alternative to rehydrate severely burned children, treat arthritic conditions, cure people of allergies. and reduce back pain associated with inflammation.

A university soccer coach was hit by a ball during a game and suffered slippage of the vertebra and a lumbar disc injury with nerve involvement in the right leg. After two weeks in bed he could only crawl to the bathroom. He then started taking enzymes and soon noticed that almost all of the pain had disappeared and he could stand erect without problem. His doctor was amazed at the patient's "remarkable" recovery and even though enzymes cannot ultimately cure his back problem, they reduced the inflammation and helped eliminate the pain. Dr. Edward Howell, author and researcher of enzymes and nutrition for over fifty years, concludes that many, if not all degenerative diseases are caused by the excessive use of enzyme-deficient cooked and processed foods. He states "the length of life is inversely proportional to the rate of exhaustion of the enzyme potential of an organism. The more the body's enzyme power must be used for digestion, the less there is for running the body."

Like money, enzymes are a form of power. They are active protein molecule catalysts, acting like microscopic hands performing literally all functions in the body. Vitamins and minerals have no function unless enzymes are present, because they are used by the enzymes to get the job done. Enzymes are present wherever chemical changes take place rapidly, without the added stimulus of heat. Since everything that takes place in physiology involves chemical change, enzymes must be present everywhere.

Your body cannot make vitamins and minerals, but it does have the power to make enzymes, which are energized protein molecules; the construction workers in the body that build the structure and keep it repaired. There are three primary groups of enzymes: **metabolic enzymes** that catalyze various chemical reactions within the cells such as detoxification and energy production; **digestive enzymes** that are secreted along the gastrointestinal tract to break down food allowing nutrient absorption and include ptyalin, pepsin, trypsin, lipase, protease and amylase; raw **plant nzymes** being protease, amylase, lipase and cellulase, contained within the plant and used to digest that particular food.

Naturally-occurring enzymes in <u>raw</u> food are activated by the moisture and heat introduced during chewing. After this initial pre-digestion, the food moves to the upper stomach where it continues to break down remaining in this location for an hour before gastric secretions move in. At this point the enzymatic action is disabled by the acids and doesn't kick in again until the food reaches the small intestine where pH is more akaline. The presence of plant enzymes can be specific as protease breaks down protein into amino acids, amylase breaks down carbohydrates into sugars, lipase breaks down fats into essential fatty acids and cellulase breaks down digestible fiber. Every raw food contains exactly the right amount and types of enzymes to digest that particular food. "An apple a day, keeps the doctor away" is definitely helpful because of the nutrients supplied, but enzymes provided are actually only digesting the apple.

Certain enzymes need the proper pH range (acid/akaline balance) to work. The pH range of the human gastrointestinal tract is approximately 1.5-8.0. Hydrochloric Acid (HCI) pH is 1.0, mixed with food it rises to 3.0. Its function is to maintain an acid pH so that the proteolytic enzymes, pepsin, produced in the stomach can work. Pancreatic (animal) enzymes work in a range of 7.8-8.3 and only provides digestive activity when the small intestine reaches 7.8, which is not often attained due to inadequate secretion of bicarbonate. Concentrated plant enzymes work in a very broad range of 3.0-9.0 and therefore are the most effective type for supplementation.

Because our diets today consist mainly of cooked and processed foods, the body may have to supply enzymes for digestion. Storing foods at cold temperature make enzymes

43

hibernate, only to be 'woken up' once they are warmed. The optimal temperature for enzyme activation is 92-104°F whereas cooking (above 118°) destroys enzymes.. If the cooked food has no enzymes, the body must produce it's own in order to digest the food. This also applies to foods that have been canned or processed (which is almost all commercially produced foods). If you just take inventory of what you eat in a particular day, I think you would be surprised at how much you depend on your body to produce enzymes to digest your meals and snacks.

When the products of incompletely digested food molecules are absorbed into the blood through a 'leaky gut', the immune system doesn't recognize this particulate, (antigens), and treats is as the enemy, increasing its number of white blood cells. Enzymes are then released from these cells, as well as the lymphatic tissue and spleen (where they are stored) in order to digest the food, an abnormal function that the immune system shouldn't have to perform. If this condition becomes chronic, the body will create physical reactions which are identified as 'food allergies'. When the white blood cells are continually elevated due to a diet in enzyme deficient foods, the immune system is weakened because the infection fighting enzymes are now trying to digest food!

If you breathe environmental pollution, ingest toxins through the skin or eat cooked foods, enzymes are required to digest whatever is taken into the body. When inflammatory conditions show up, including food and environmental allergies, they may stem from enzyme deficiencies which began months before. Lita Lee in Earth letter, Vol. 2, No. 1, mentioned seeing not only children and adults, but also nursing babies with severe environmental allergies manifesting as swollen, red, runny eyes and nose. Their symptoms were relieved within hours

44

of ingesting a NUTRI-ESSENCE enzyme formula, containing food enzymes, Rose hips, Alfalfa, Mullein and Echinacea. This particular combination also was helpful in reducing morning sickness in pregnant women.

Enzymes that are used up in the digestion of food, cause the enzyme storage banks to become depleted. Viruses, bacteria and Candida yeast organisms can now have a field day because their exterminators are out feasting on food particles. The pancreas can produce digestive enzymes to digest the cooked food, although it was not designed to work overtime. Eventually the pancreas loses the ability to make enzymes, and degenerative disease sets in.

The size and weight of the pancreas will vary due to diet. The more this organ must work to compensate for enzyme deficient foods, the larger it gets. It must send messages to all parts of the body looking for enzymes it can recycle, and changing these metabolic enzymes into digestive enzymes takes a lot of work for this organ. The enlargement may not harm the pancreas, but when it confiscates metabolic enzymes, it deprives the body by restricting the mechanics that every organ and cell needs to carry on its functions.

Eating raw foods definitely has its advantages for many reasons, but in some instances, specific enzymes may not be released. For example, inhibited enzyme of wheat is amylase, potato is invertase and trypsin, barley is trypsin, rye is protease and sunflower seed is trypsin. Enzyme inhibitors are nature's way of protecting a plant. They keep enzymes inactive until such time as the seed, nut, grain or bean is ready for germination. This is why squirrels bury nuts. They instinctively know their nutrients are more bioavailable to the body when the enzymes are released, so they wait to eat them until just the right time. These type of raw foods require enzyme supplementation or you can wait until they begin sprouting to eat them.

Many people who avoid meat and dairy want to assure themselves of adequate calcium and protein and therefore have switched to soy products. There are some different views on soy although most recognize the nutritious advantage this bean gives you. Raw soybeans do contain enzyme inhibitors which block the action of trypsin and other enzymes. These anti-nutrients are not completely deactivated during ordinary cooking and those remaining may produce gastric distress, reduced protein digestion and chronic deficiencies in amino acid uptake. The protease inhibitors may have a beneficial side, as laboratory experiments have found they inhibit some types of cancer. In fermented soy (tempe, natto and miso) more of the enzyme inhibitors are deactivated and seem to pose no harm.

Trypsin inhibitors and hemagglutinin in the blood, are growth depressants, not only affecting the hair but also may restrict the normal development of children's bodies. This combination can lead to enlargement of the pancreas as the body try's to compensate by producing its own enzymes. A Fermented soy drink (recently being marketed) and fermented soy products have most of the enzyme inhibitors missing, because the bean has in effect begun to 'sprout'. Also, any of the soy products that have been cooked have killed a good many of the enzyme inhibitors along with the enzymes, therefore if you decide to include soy in your diet, take supplemental enzymes with your foods.

Soybeans are also high in phytates, an organic acid present in seed hulls, which blocks the uptake of essential minerals (magnesium, calcium, iron and zinc) in the intestinal tract. In persons with high iron, phytates will bind the iron in the intestines and may actually have the beneficial effect of inhibiting cancer. Non meat-eaters are more prone to deficiencies caused by phytates, because when soy products are consumed with meat, the mineral blocking effects of the phytates are now reduced. Since soy is in so many food products from baby formulas to additives (like soy protein isolate and textured vegetable protein), you may want to do further research on both sides of the soy issue, before deciding on whether to ingest unfermented soy products.

Starch blockers, a recent diet fad, are actually enzyme inhibitors working on preventing starch from being assimilated. Although this may cause weight reduction, this process takes its toll on the pancreas, that must work overtime to provide enzymes to digest the starch. These blockers also cause a great quantity of enzymes to be excreted through the urine. Using starch blockers can definitely shorten your lifetime through enzyme depletion. Food additives can also destroy enzymes, particularly catalase, found in almost all living cells of plants and animals, and man. Catalase controls cell respiration and sets up a barrier to virus infections, cancer and certain poisons.

Enzymes can't work alone and most require the presence of vitamins and minerals, known as co-enzymes, in order to do their work. Co-enzymes cannot be made by the body. For example, vitamins A, D, E, and K require fat for absorption and in order to be broken down, they need the enzyme, lipase. If it is deficient, fat will not be digested and absorbed, and the vitamins will not be released. Water soluble vitamin B's and C, also help enzymes do their job. Vitamin C is necessary for the enzyme that helps make collagen, a major component of skin. Minerals and electrolytes are necessary because they are part of the enzyme structure. For instance, Zinc is part of more than two hundred enzymes and helps to metabolize food. It also is critical for the proper functioning of superoxide dismutase (S.O.D.), an enzyme that fights free radicals. So you see, that if enzymes are not present, the vitamins and minerals have no reason to be in the body.

Antioxidant enzymes are the first line of defense against free radical pathology. When the levels of free radicals are greater than the supply of antioxidant enzymes the result is a free radical pathology (ie., cancer, heart disease, etc.). Free radical damage to certain types of cells is irreversible. Heart muscle cells, nerve cells including brain cells and certain sensor cells of the immune system cannot be replaced in the adult human. Damage to these cells must be prevented through use of S.O.D. along with Catalase, Glutathione Peroxidase and Methionine Reductase are enzymes that do not digest foods, but convert free radicals back into the original materials, oxygen and water. S.O.D. will not work without Catalase and when combined, are effective free-radical converters that detoxify the body without the usual cleansing symptoms.

Glutathione Peroxidase consists of the amino acid glutathione and trace mineral selenium. It has been described as the best anti-aging agent naturally produced by the body. Free radical cross linking produces skin wrinkles and this enzyme is effective in approving skin appearance, shrinking moles and making age spots disappear. It also helps chemically sensitive people control their allergies and build resistance to the effects of pollution. Methionine Reductase is an excellent enzyme to combat chemical poisoning from carbon monoxide, insecticides, air pollution, etc. It has detoxifying abilities of free radical toxins generated by mercury dental fillings.

Antioxidant enzymes work synergistically with other enzymes and co-factors. Isolated enzymes cannot duplicate this complex interaction. For this reason, the only way to insure that all antioxidant enzymes factors and co-factors are available for the body to use, is to provide the complete organic complex as exists only in living foods.   Botanists have developed several unique strains of enzyme-rich IsoSproutPlex™. Not only have these "supersprouts" demonstrated high levels of antioxidant enzymes, but the have shown the remarkable ability to enhance the body's own production of antioxidant enzymes.

Enzymes can play a big role in anti-aging skin care. Trypsin, pancreatin and keratinase are used to break down and dissolve dead skin cells. Papain, from young green papaya plants, has the ability to dissolve and digest old, debilitated or dead cells from the outer layer of the skin without harming the new cells. Green papaya enzymes assist the healing of uneven pigmentation, fine lines and brown spots by fighting free radical damage and boosting cell production. They are sometimes considered an natural alternative to Retin-A.

Research has turned up evidence that enzyme-replacement therapy can affect disease. The Bircher-Benner Sanitarium in Switzerland noted great success with enzyme therapy for diabetes, ulcers, Graves disease asthma and arthritis. Impaired enzyme activity, especially lipase, may be the cause of certain cardiovascular diseases because lipase stripped fats from cooking or processing, causes cholesterol deposits to form in the arteries. When lipase deficient fat meets hydrochloric acid in the human stomach, it is identified by the body in such a way that it is not digested. Thus it may be improperly metabolized when it reaches the body tissue later.

A woman is Illinois reported miraculous changes in her son who has Muscular Dystrophy and is mentally retarded. The only change she made to his diet was adding the enzyme formulation PROZYME™/ TYME ZYME™ at every meal. After five weeks his pain was gone, the aged look he had developed, disappeared and his energy level increased to where he was getting out of a chair easier and walking faster. His interest in life came back and the tremors in his hands lessened. Scientific testing was done that proved the absorption of nutrients were increased with the bioengineered enzymes. The woman is convinced that the enzymes helped her son's body fight the disease.

Blood tests done in 1958 by L.O. Pilgeram of Stanford University demonstrated that there is a progressive decline in lipase in the blood of atherosclerosis patients with advancing middle and old age. Lipase, present in butter, unpasteurized milk, olives, flax seeds, poultry and animal fat is also the enzyme found to be deficient in obese people. Indications show that when fats, whether animal or vegetable, are eaten along with their associated enzymes, no harmful effect on the arteries or heart results.

Arthritis has been called the 'cooked food' disease. After a study done in Manchester, England scientists concluded that rheumatoid arthritis might be a deficiency disease arising from the inability of the body to deal adequately with protein digestion and metabolism. After 292 people were treated with enzymes, 264 showed improvement of various degrees. This type of success occurs over a long period of time and therefore is less attractive than pain killing drugs, but it also may solve the problem, permanently.

Enzymes are prescribed in medicine to digest blood clots and blocked vessels, clean up debris around infection and are used for abscesses around catheters, valves and graphs. They are safe and effective for all people including the elderly and babies. Researchers have found that enzymes can make leukemic cells return to normal cells and help cause the demise of cancer cells. Dr. Sherry Rogers saw a friend reduce a liver painfully swollen with cancer, by using enzyme therapy. She discovered numerous reports of people who used enzymes to clear metastatic cancer after the were diagnosed as terminal. As in any therapy, massive doses of enzymes should be taken under advisement from a health practitioner.

Athlete's are particularly susceptible to enzyme deficiency. The more they exercise, the more they eat and if they do not follow a raw food diet, they will use metabolic enzymes for digestion. This leaves fewer enzymes for organ and blood processes necessary for nutritional balance that contributes to the success of an athlete's performance.

Stress plays a big part in enzyme deficiency. Emotional problems, worry, fear, loneliness, even the stress of a physical problem, like getting dentures, can interfere with the secretion of digestive enzymes. This results in their decrease in tissue and fluids which can cause the skin to wrinkle and shrivel, hair to thin, muscles to sag, eyes to lose sparkle and vitality to diminish. Stress and enzyme deficiency may be a contributing factor towards premature aging.

You can't get enough enzymes. There are no synthetic enzymes. Only living matter can product them and because plant enzymes work in a wider range of pH found in the digestive tract, they are better all around enzymes than animal based types. Supplements of plant enzymes help food to be assimilated in order to repair organs, glands, bones, muscles and nerves. Any excess is stored in the liver and the muscles. Like any addition to the body, tread lightly when first adding enzymes to your diet.

One of the jobs of enzymes is to act as house cleaners for the body, therefore the addition of enzymes may cause an initial throwing off of toxins. This can result in intensification of symptoms, a "healing crisis". Some people get a skin rash as the toxins try to work their way out. As in any detoxification and rebuilding program start out slowly and consult a health practitioner. Our advice is to consider taking enzymes every time you eat ANYTHING! that is not raw. You will be surprised at how you can throw all of your antacids away. If you ever eat that big holiday dinner again and feel bloated and exhausted after the meal, you probably forgot to take your enzymes. Remember, you are not what you eat, but what you assimilate!

Recommended reading:

Enzyme Nutrition, by Dr. Edward, Howell, Avery Publishing,

ESSENTIAL FATTY ACIDS...

As we age we want our quality of life to improve or at least not deteriorate. Degenerative diseases that involve fat metabolism have been increasing throughout this century. In the early 1900's, people died of bacterial infections, poor surgical procedures, etc. but by the year 2000 it is expected that over half of American deaths will be caused by arterial, vascular and coronary heart disease. Fats have been implicated as one of the causes for this dilemma and the craze is on to eat fat-free. Low fat diets may actually speed up the degenerative process because they are low in healthy promoting essential fatty acids as well as having high levels of damaging saturated and trans-fat laden fats.

Recent discoveries by Dr. Robert I-San Lin revealed that a prime suspect in the growth of cancer cells is a fat imbalance, not an overabundance of fats in general. Through experimentation he found that arachidonic acid, an essential fatty acid of the Omega-6 variety, can actually promote cancer cell growth. Arachidonic acid is required for animals to grow. Normal cells divide and multiply up to a point at which stage they, in most cases, only replace those that have died. If this did not happen, our cells would engulf our bodies. When the Omega-6 is not balanced by Omega-3, these cells don't know when to stop. When those cells are cancerous, this becomes a dangerous condition.

Since arachidonic acid only exists in animal bodies, when they eat feed containing large amounts of soybean and corn, their Omega-6 production goes up. When people eat these animals they develop an essential fatty acid imbalance, unless they are also eating plants high in Omega-3. During the last dozen years, garlic has been shown to modulate arachidonic acid metabolism and it is suggested that it may modulate the cancer risk if these essential fats are out of balance.

Fats come from animal and plant sources and usually take a solid form. Oils are produced mainly from plants and remain liquid. Fats and oils are both made of fatty acid molecules. Saturated fatty acid molecules are shaped like a straight line so they remain in a compact mass, staying hard at room temperature (butter). Monounsaturated fatty acids have a single "kink" in their molecular make up which makes them more fluid (Olive and canola oils). These seem to play a beneficial role in the management of blood cholesterol and therefore heart disease.

Polyunsaturated fatty acid molecules have two "kinks" which not only makes them more fluid, but more likely to spoil easily (Safflower and corn oil). Superunsaturated fatty acids are molecules with three "kinks" and carry the most nutrients (black currant, flax, primrose oil). They also are most susceptible to spoilage and should be kept in a cool, dark place.

All of these fats are natural, but there's a fifth type of fat that's manufactured and these are suspected to be the leading cause of health problems associated with fats. This process makes the fat more stable, and is popular with food manufacturers who do not have to refrigerate the oils. The chemical refining process used to make a hydrogenated oil is simple. Hydrogen is reacted with the liquid oil, using a catalyst such as nickel, zinc or copper. This substance becomes a smoky mass of grease after which they degum the oils with phosphoric acid, which at the same time, removes several health promoting substances such as lecithin, chlorophyll and trace minerals. They are then bleached and recolored to look like butter. This method converts healthy "cis-fatty acid" to a "trans-fatty acid". They can also occur naturally in cow's milk with up to 14% butter fat.

The main sources of synthetic trans-fats are from margarine, shortening, deep fried foods cooked in partially hydrogenated high-heated oils, processed animal products and anytime partially hydrogenated is included in packaged foods (cookies, chips, bread, etc.). The head of Harvard School of Medicine, Dr. Walter Willet stated that the harmful effects of trans-fat laden margarine on the heart is connected to deaths from heart disease. Our bodies can handle an occasional ingestion of trans-fat foods, but over a lifetime, these unnatural substances accumulate and interfere with the normal biological chemistry of our bodies, create corrupted organs and muscles and cause cells to lose their DNA reproductive integrity, which promotes aging and degenerative disease.

Trans fats can decrease testosterone production, promote pregnancy complications and low birth weight babies, promote diabetes and cancer, alter the immune function and taxes the liver's ability to process toxins. Researchers at the Harvard Medical School did a study of 85,000 female nurses over the course of eight years. They discovered that the women with the highest trans-fat intake had a 50% higher rate of heart attacks and coronary artery disease.

Trans-fats like hydrogenated soybean and tropical palm kernel oil are solid at body temperature thereby remaining sticky and are likely to clog our arteries. They also interfere with prostaglandin production (hormone like regulators in the blood) and kidney functions as well as promote ulcers. Unnatural trans-fats disrupt the body's metabolism by changing the permeability of cells to let in viruses, toxins and parasites. This syndrome is called "leaky gut". Cholesterol levels also reflect elevations in the "bad" LDL when trans-fats are consumed for as little as a three week period. If this substance is eliminated from the diet, the cell's fluid membrane will be able to transport and metabolize excess sugars, fats and toxins, and help to cleanse the body.

It is important to use oils in as natural a state as possible. This not only means refraining from using hydrogenated oil, but also being aware of how the oil was extracted. Most mass market oils are refined, being obtained by chemical solvent extraction at a temperature of 500°F. These solvents may be carcinogenic and the high temperatures "kill" many of the nutrients. Expeller pressed oils are produced through a chemical-free mechanical process which limits temperatures to 185°F. Cold pressed oils also use a mechanical process in which temperatures are restricted to 120° F allowing more of the nutrients to remain in tact. The higher the temperature used in the extraction process, the lower the nutrient quality of the oil. Refined olive oil loses over 100 volatile compounds that gives it a distinctive taste. Oils should be labeled "cold pressed" or "virgin" for maximum quality.

One of the best oils for health is olive oil. It protects against heart disease and is implicated in cancer prevention. It also contributes to blood sugar control, essential for diabetics. Make sure olive oil is labeled "virgin" to be sure you are getting an unrefined nutritious product. ("Pure" labels are still a refined product.)

When we consume refined polyunsaturated oils on a regular basis, we can create an environment for cancer to develop. Immune system function is being suppressed by an imbalance in the ratio of omega-6 to omega-3 oils, thereby restricting the body's ability to fight disease. These essential fatty acids (EFA's) were discovered at the University of Minnesota by George and Mildred Burr in 1929. They cannot be made by the body, but must be taken in with food.

EFAs are the foremen in the body's workforce. They are

required for the formation of prostaglandins which are hormone-like substances that "tell" cells when to divide or not to divide, when to take in nutrients, when to expel waste products, when to lay down bone or absorb bone, when to wake up or sleep, to feel pain, to form a clot, etc. Without prostaglandins the body would be totally discombobulated! Without EFAs prostaglandins would be on a permanent vacation. Essential fatty acid therapy should also include a broad spectrum of vitamins and minerals. The cofactors of EFA metabolism are vitamins C, E, A, betacarotene, biotin, B3, B6 and the minerals Zinc and Magnesium.

Problems that can be associated with essential fatty acid deficiency are skin and airway membrane damage, suppression of the immune system, brittle nails, dry skin, hair loss, depression, tinitus, cold intolerance, chronic pain, asthma, irritable bowel syndrome, heart disease, migraines and arthritis. If you experience any of these symptoms you may want to analyze your diet to see if you are lacking EFAs or are eating foods to create an EFA imbalance.

EFAs play a big part in maintaining the structure of the cells and of producing energy in the body. When they are not balanced they compromise health. Omega-6 fatty acids (linoleic acid) is found in vegetable oils and bee pollen. It is consumed in great quantities and rarely a deficiency is seen in normal diets. Omega-3 (alpha-linolenic acid) tends to be a casualty of processing of oils and foods, but is found in flax and fish oils predominantly, although trace amounts can be found in canola oil, soybean oil and walnut oil.

One of the best nutritional sources of Omega-3 is flax. It can reverse the degenerative process. The EFAs prevent heart disease by thinning the blood and removing cholesterol. They also normalize the immune system response by subtly affecting the production of prostaglandins and leukotrienes, two body chemicals made from fatty acids. One of the primary good side effects of taking flax is that it is an internal wrinkle cream. By providing moisture and necessary oils from the inside, the skin becomes softer and wrinkles seem to fill in and lessen.

Since we want to create a balance in essential fatty acids, adding flax to your diet is an easy fix. Flax can be purchased as oils, capsules, flaxmeal or you can grind your own flaxseed. Flax is a source of lignin, a plant compound that our body converts to lignan, anti-carcinogenic, antifungal and antiviral substances that we synthesize in our bowels when bacteria breaks down plant food in the digestive tract. All vegetables provide lignan precursors, but flax provides 800mg per gram as compared to only 8 mg per gram from other fiber sources. Flax fiber can protect against colon cancer and breast cancer by flushing excess estrogen and other carcinogens out of the body.

Gamma-linoleic acid (GLA) is identical to Omega-3 fatty acids except for its bonding structure and therefore gives similar health benefits. GLA can be found in borage(24%), black currant (18%) and evening primrose oils (9%), but unless they are cold pressed, they may contain pesticides or solvents. If you eat saturated fats or refined vegetable oils, you may block the body's natural ability to create GLA from linoleic acids. Other GLA blockers are sugar, virus infections, dietary deficiencies and diabetes. Supplementation is absolutely necessary if you are not eating right, have liver problems, inflammatory disease or experience PMS.

Essential fatty acids should be an important part of your diet especially if you exercise, as EFAs help the cells to recover from muscle use and overuse. They are needed by our glands to carry out the secretion of hormones and other regulating substances and are essential to infant pre-natal and post-natal development. You should take inventory of your eating habits and consider supplementation with Omega-3 products. You will definitely see a change in the texture of your skin and notice a reduction in the depth of lines in your face, and if nothing else, this is worth it!

One very important reason for men to avoid trans fats and balance EFAs is that baldness may be avoided. A report on the correlation between heart attacks and baldness, reveals that the gunk created by trans fats adheres to both the arterial wall and hair follicles. This plaque builds up smothering the hair and preventing it from getting oxygen. Thus hair actually stops growing because it is buried under layers of fatty goo, (ever see a bald man with a dull head?). Once these layers are cleaned off and the trans fats eliminated from the diet, dormant hair may actually emerge in tact, or new growth will be regenerated. Predisposition's to hair loss from "genetic" reasons may be accelerated or diminished if men will avoid hats that make their head sweat, keep the scalp clean and avoid trans fat causing foods.

Since people are eating more and more cooked or processed meals, they are not getting the nutrients as nature provides in raw foods. Beneficial vitamins and minerals necessary for a youthful appearance and healthy body, are found in dark colored green vegetables. As we get older and "abuse" our bodies, we are less resistant to degenerative disease. Part of staying "young" is to prevent the acceleration of this aspect of the aging process and consuming raw greens or supplements will definitely keep time on your side.

Many years ago, Dr. G.H. Earp-Thomas, in his quest for duplicating an electrolyte formula, worked with wheat grasses. He discovered that the grasses contained a unique, electrical magnetic energy. The relatively high level of the electrical energy force transferred from the earth's magnetic field, is sent via these same live grasses. Walking on bare earth, links us to this energy source. This aids immensely to our body's magnetic, electrical "battery" so critically necessary for good health. (Take note that the Indians normally went without coverings on their feet. Shoes create insulated barriers and prevent this energy from being absorbed by the body. Coming to the U.S. market soon, are *Biolex* footwear, that link the body's neurological system to ground exchanging static electricity for the earth's natural energy.) Live plants transfer this energy from the earth, therefore when you eat raw greens you receive the benefit of highly energized foods, necessary to keep you at your optimal best.

Bill Rodgers, 47, is the four-time winner of the New York and Boston marathons and holds sixteen U.S. single-age masters records for the 5k, 8k, 10k half-marathon and 30k. He says, "You can get away with 'nutritional murder' in your youth, but the onset of age requires employing every possible advantage to keep yourself physically afloat. Distance running is extremely demanding (I still race twenty five times a year), which is why I rely on powdered extracts from whole food ingredients such as barley grass, to help me perform in the sport at the highest level possible."

Green foods can also strengthen the immune system by providing the nutrients needed for the synthesis of the immune cells. Greens also contain an anti-peptic ulcer factor, protect our bodies from the effects of radiation, lower serum cholesterol, support healthy blood and circulation as well as helping to maintain proper operation of the intestinal tract. They are nature's vitamin pill, providing C, A, iron, folic acid, protein, B12, K and calcium.

Dr. Benjamin Lau, MD, Ph.D. from California's Loma Linda University Medical School found that barley grass, wheat grass and Chlorella are all potent stimulators of macrophages which play a vital role in the immune system. When small quantities of these compounds are present, the macrophages produce powerful chemical substances that are known to kill bacteria, viruses and cancer cells. This may also be the reason that Japanese women who include seaweed in their diet have fewer incidents of breast cancer than their counterparts eating "western-style" meals.

"Green" eating can promote longevity and resistance to disease. A report in the American Journal of Clinical Nutrition, (41:32-36) indicates that elderly people are the least likely group to die from cancer if their diet contains an abundance of green and yellow vegetables. Cereal grasses contain strong anti-cancer agents such as the anti-oxidant vitamins E and A, Zinc and the trace mineral selenium. Antitumor effects in animals have also been demonstrated by an intake of Chlorella, Kelp and chlorophyll. "Green" eating can promote longevity and resistance to disease. Young barley leaves and wheat grass are good natural sources of chlorophyll, minerals (particularly high in calcium, magnesium and potassium,), vitamins and enzymes needed for proper metabolism of our body cells. The Japanese claim that daily consumption of cereal grass juice and Chlorella helps reverse the aging process due to the high enzyme and anti-oxidant activity of the juice.

Studies showed that several green vegetables provide anti-mutagenic protection from a number of cancer causing chemicals. This activity was found to be proportional to the concentration of chlorophyll in the vegetables (darker green is better). Chlorophyll has been called "concentrated sun power". It is the outcome of photosynthesis and in wheat grass juice, accounts for 70% of the solid content. Chlorophyll is to the plant as blood is to the animals. Long known only as a disinfectant, chlorophyll is a natural blood builder and also heals wounds by stimulating repair of damaged tissues and inhibiting growth of bacteria. It is effective in speeding the healing of peptic ulcers, diseases of the colon, and treating pancreatitis and kidney stones.

Chlorophyll has been known to cure acute infections of the respiratory tract and controls halitosis and oral diseases. This antioxidant has even been shown to nullify the effects of a variety of environmental and food substances (such as cigarette smoke, diesel fumes, coal dust, and fried beef), which are known to cause mutation. It can actually be more effective than vitamin A, C or E antioxidants. Chlorophyll therapy provides an excellent alternative to drug therapy because repeated tests have shown it produces virtually no toxic side effects.

One major advantage that chlorophyll provides to the body, is its ability to help alkalize the pH in the blood.

When pH is too acid, free radicals reign, anti-oxidants are immobilized and therefore cannot do their job of attacking invaders. The body tends to buffer this acidity with sodium, causing stomach upset, and also calls upon its next buffer, calcium which is drawn from the bones and placed into the blood. Calcium lodges in the bloodstream and sets the stage for arthritis, therefore it is absolutely necessary to add chlorophyll foods to your diet to help balance the pH.

More recently, researchers have focused their interest on radioprotective, antimutagenic and anticarcinogenic effects of chlorophylls. They have been shown to nullify the effects of a variety of environmental and food substances which are known to cause mutation (change of DNA). This is one of the reasons why scientists today are recommending inclusion in the diet of green leafy vegetables containing chlorophyll and other cancer preventative substances.

When adding greens to your diet you may consider cereal grasses and seaweed along with the dark leafy veggies harvested from your organic garden. Pesticides are not beneficial to health, therefore whenever possible, insist on organic food and/or supplements. Dehydrated cereal grasses such as wheatgrass and barley grass contain highly concentrated amounts of necessary nutrients and may be the answer to high paced lifestyles where more concentrated stores of energy are required.

A fact little understood by meat and dairy consumers, is that vegetarianism does not necessarily lead to protein deficiency. A grain and vegetable centered diet, including wheat or barley grass, may actually result in a higher intake of protein than a meat based diet. Dehydrated cereal grasses contain 25% protein whereas milk (3%), eggs (12%) and steak (16%) are all lower! Even bee pollen contains five to seven times more protein than beef, eggs and cheese of equal weight. Adequate protein is necessary for the formation of essential compounds including antibodies, hormones, neurotransmitters and enzymes and for the growth of all tissues and replacement of damaged tissues. It also is an important source of food energy and helps maintain the electrolyte/water balance and pH.

Vegetable proteins have been considered incomplete (not containing all 20 amino acids) and therefore cannot be optimally used by the body like animal food proteins. Cereal grass is different according to Pines, manufacturers of wheat and barley grass supplements, claiming they contain all the essential amino acids in amounts which make its protein usable in the body. From a protein standpoint, cereal grass must be an important part of all non-animal based diets

Harvesting cereal grasses at the right time is important because they go through several stages as they grow, where their chemical and nutritional profiles vary widely. In the early stages they store large amounts of chlorophyll, vitamins and proteins. If cut or eaten at this stage, they will grow again. During the next stage (jointing) the grass begins to form a stem which is the peak of a cereal plant's vegetative development. After the jointing stage, the stem forms branches and continues to grow increasing cellulose levels while decreasing chlorophyll, protein and vitamins. Once this stage is reached the plant should not be harvested until it produces seed because it will not regenerate itself. Dried barley grass juice harvested at the proper time, can have five times the iron in spinach, seven times the vitamin C in oranges and an abundance of bioflavonoids which can slow down cellular oxidation (aging). It is optimal to harvest cereal grass during the first stage to reap maximum nutritional benefits from the growing cycle, therefore question supplement suppliers to determine if these criteria have been met.

ANALYSIS OF DEHYDRATED CEREAL GRASS (1 tsp powder)

Vtamins:		Minerals:	
A	1750 I/U	Calcium	18 mg
K	280 mcg	Phosphorus	18 mg
C	11 mg	Potassium	112 mg
E	1.1 mcg	Magnesium	2.6 mg
B-12	1 mcg	Iron	2 mg
Thiamin	10 mcg	Manganese	.35 mg
Choline	1 mg	Selenium	3.5 mcg
Riboflavin	71 mcg	Sodium	1.0 mg
Pyridoxine	45 mcg	Zinc	17.5mcg
Niacin	263 mcg	Iodine	7.0 mcg
Pantothenic	84 mcg	Copper	.02 mg
Biotin	4 mcg	Cobalt	1.75mcg
Folic Acid	38 mcg		

Amino Acids:			
Lysine	29 mg	Leucine	31 mg
Histidine	16 mg	Tyrosine	18 mg
Arginine	39 mg	Serine	85 mg
Asparatic Acid	78 mg	Methionine	15 mg
Threonine	37 mg	Cystine	8 mg
Glutamic Acid	85 mg	Tryptophan	4 mg
Proline	33 mg	Amide	10 mg
Glycine	41 mg	Purines	2 mg
Alanine	48 mg		
Valine	44 mg	**PROTEIN**	800 mg
Isoleucine	31 mg	**CHLOROPHYLL**	19 mg

In addition to cereal grasses and dark greens, sea vegetables, algae and Chlorella play an important role in micronutrient assimilation. Years of intense farming methods have leached adequate levels of micronutrients (trace elements essential for normal growth and development) from our soils, leaving the foods grown on those soils, deficient. When micronutrients are added back into a diet, people often find that in addition to having more

66

energy overall, immunity is boosted, resulting in an increased ability to cope with stress and to ward off infection. In addition, chronic allergies and asthma may disappear seemingly overnight. The skin becomes clear and bright, hair becomes thicker and shinier, and fingernails grow longer and stronger. Micronutirent consumption has also been linked to a decrease in symptoms of PMS and cystic breast disease.

In addition to improving the condition of already existing hair, micronutrient supplementation has also been responsible for hair re-growth and re-pigmentation of gray hair. A documented case history describes a young girl in Connecticut who suffered from alopecia (baldness). A noted children's hospital prescribed different shampoos and when they had no effect, the doctors said her condition was stress related and gave up on her. A hairdresser suggested she add SOURCE micronutrients to her diet and within four months hair started growing back on her head. To date she is about to throw her wig away! In a test case, a horse was give micronutrients for warts and a poor hoof condition. What they didn't expect, was for his gray hair to turn color again as a result of the treatment. This gives a clue to the fact that some cases of gray hair may be attributed to lack of essential nutrients in our diets.

Sea vegetables have received a reprieve from man's destruction (so far). They are high in minerals particularly calcium, iodine, potassium and magnesium. Kelp is high in minerals, particularly calcium, iodine, potassium, and magnesium. It is also a good source of Vitamin C. Kelp sparks vital enzyme reactions and increases thyroid metabolism so it may be effective in weight control. Kelp has been used in folk medicine to treat respiratory, gastrointestinal and genitourinary problems and has been shown to lower blood pressure and cholesterol. In animal tests, Dr. Jane Teas, found that feeding rats with kelp significantly delays and reduces the development of breast cancer induced by chemical carcinogens. It is speculated that kelp contains compounds which may counteract carcinogens or cancer producing substances and others suggest it may act through modulating the immune system.

Chlorella is a single cell, globular green, water borne algae, that is the largest selling health food supplement in Japan. It is rich in chlorophyll, minerals, vitamins A, B3, B2, B6, pantotheic acid, folic acid, choline, biotin, lypoic acid, nucleic acid and other substances that provide various biological effects. It is high in protein (see chart), has 800 times as much vitamin C as milk and is reported to have the ability to stimulate the immune system. It isn't the amount of protein in Chlorella that makes a difference in our health but the kind of protein it is. One gram provides 667 mg. of protein, but this includes 29.5 mg. of RNA and 2.8 mg. of DNA which helps maintain cellular protection and boost energy levels. Chlorella does supply all the essential amino acids in good balance, and is thus an excellent whole food in itself.

Dr. Bernard Jensen in *Chlorella, Gem of the Orient*, states that "Dr. Benjamin Frank, author of *The No-Aging Diet*, suggests that human RNA/DNA production slows down as people age, resulting in lower levels of vitality and increased vulnerability to various diseases. When we eat foods rich in DNA and RNA it protects our own cellular nucleic acids, allowing the cell wall to function efficiently. As a result the cell remains clean and well nourished. The DNA and RNA found in foods that we eat does not directly replace human cellular DNA and RNA. Rather, their amino acid combinations, after digestion and assimilation, immediately provide the "building blocks" for repair of our pre-existing genetic material. Dr. Michinori Kimura found that Chlorella consists of ten percent RNA and three percent DNA which would make it the most concentrated source of nucleic acids in the world, being seventeen times more concentrated than sardines, the next best source.

Protein comparison per 100 grams	
CHLORELLA	67
CHICKEN	24
BEEF	24-27
WHEAT	13
EGGS	13
RICE	3
FISH	18-29
POTATOES	3

The Chlorella is a 2 1/2 billion year old single-cell algae that doesn't die, but instead reproduces itself into four new Chlorella cells. If we could teach the cells in our bodies to multiply rather than age and die, we could definitely prolong life. Chlorella Growth Factor (CGF) promotes this cell multiplication and prevents disease by repairing and renewing organs, glands and tissues in the body. Experiments have shown that CGF promotes faster-than-normal growth without any adverse side effects.

Chlorella cells are very tiny organisms, grown in special culture pools and should not be confused with spirulina which is a multi-cell plant with larger cells that are harvested from lakes and ponds. Chlorella has been an effective treatment for gastric and duodenal ulcers, lowering cholesterol and blood pressure, fighting cancer, warding off cold germs, aiding in intestinal peristalsis, and has been used in treatment of "incurable" wounds. It combats the effects of aging, strengthens the immune responses and promotes growth in young children and animals.

A thirty-eight year old man who was suffering from high blood pressure and impotence among a lot of other health problems, was told by his doctor to increase his intake of greens. For this patient who disliked vegetables, the doctor recommended Kyo-Green®, a powder containing Chlorella, Laminaria (kelp), young barley leaves and wheat grass (a high source of chlorophyll). Within one week the man's blood pressure had returned to normal. Within two weeks, his stamina and his sexual potency returned and many other symptoms which he had considered "just a part of life", disappeared. Two years later, he still maintained normal blood pressure and found he had fewer colds. The power of greens and seaweed can definitely make a difference.

The myth "you are what you eat" translates into "you are what you absorb". If greens only "visit" on the way from mouth to anus, you might as well not bother eating them at all. All green vegetables and cereal grasses should be consumed raw to maximize bioavailablity of the nutrients. As we discuss in the chapter on enzymes, cooked foods make the digestive system do more work, increasing the risk that the vitamins, minerals and trace elements will bypass absorption.

Plant enzyme supplements are an absolute necessity whenever cooked greens are consumed. Also, you should determine that your supplements have been processed with low or no heat, leaving the enzymes in tact, (call the manufacturer). As the years go by, the "authorities" change the food groups, but greens always remain a constant. In our estimation, they should be a major part of everyone's diet including both raw veggies and supplements containing micronutrients, cereal grasses and sea vegetables.

Since powdered greens supplementation may not be as exciting to drink as a good cup of Cappuccino, and may be even more difficult to get your child to slurp down, we have listed a few recipes for good greens drinks supplied by the manufacturers of Kyo-Green®.

All drinks using greens powder should be mixed in blender for smoothness.

Greens and Banana Smoothie
1 ripe banana, fresh or frozen
1 teaspoon greens powder
1 cup water

Variations to this recipe:
Add to mixture 2 pitted dates
and pinch of ginger

Another potent green food is Hawaiian Spirulina, considered one of the premium green superfoods. I provides exceptionally concentrated nutrition in a whole food form our bodies can very easily digest and absorb. This concentrated whole food source of phyto-nutrients can supply the body with a rich mixture of carotenoids, chlorophyll, enzymes, complete vegetarian protein, B-vitamins and a newly discovered anti-viral compound called calcium spirulan.

Blue green algae, one of 50,000 species of algae, seaweed and plankton, is also a nutrient dense food and only a small amount is necessary to supply the body with a little of almost every nutrient that it needs. It provides biologically active vitamins, minerals, trace elements, amino acids, simple carbohydrates, enzymes, fatty acids, carotenoids, and chlorophyll. It's protein content is of a type called glycoproteins which is more easily broken down and assimilated by the body than lipoproteins found in vegetables and meat. Algae and sea vegetables are used for healing purposes throughout the world and should be part of everyone's diet.

Recommended Reading:

Chlorella, Jewel of the Far East, By Bernard Jensen, Ph.D.

GARLIC..

They say you can tell an Italian by the garlic on his breath, but you can bet he's a lot healthier because of it. For over 5,000 years garlic has been used in health care, mostly in the pure or raw bulb state. As far back as 1500 B.C., the Egyptians used garlic as an effective remedy for many ailments including heart problems and tumors and it has long been considered a heart remedy in Ayurvedic medicine. Garlic has been purported to have healing power in the treatment of hypertension, arthritis, heavy metal poisoning, constipation and athlete's foot.

In the last 20 years over 1800 scientific papers have been published on various aspects of garlic research. This magnificent food has the ability to decrease the levels of "bad" cholesterol while raising the levels of "good" cholesterol. The Danish and Russians have used garlic for centuries for coughs and colds. Grandmothers have been telling us to gargle with garlic to relieve a sore throat or to apply garlic juice to ward off wound infections. Garlic is a natural antibiotic!

A study by the People's Republic of China reported residents of Cangshan County had a lower death rate due to stomach cancer than those living in the county of Qixia. They discovered that the Cangshan County residents regularly ate 20 grams of garlic per day whereas the Qixia residents ate very little. The reasoning behind the success of garlic in cancer prevention was attributed to the levels of nitrites in their gastric juices. Nitrites are the precursors of carcinogens and the Cangshan residents who ate garlic had lower levels of nitrites, therefore inhibiting the growth of cancer. Dr. Jinzhou Liu, a Chinese biochemist from Penn State University, proved that Kyolic® Aged Garlic Extract™ was more effective than Vitamin C in preventing nitrosamines from forming in laboratory experiments. Nirtrosamines are one of the world's most potent known carcinogens.

Garlic has been thought of as a miracle cure. It is effective against forms of Staph, Strep, Bacillus and Salmonella and scores of other infectious agents. It is antibacterial, antifungal, antiviral and antiparasitic. Dr. Albert Schweitzer had success using it to treat typhus, cholera and typhoid. In China, eleven patients who had crypto-coccal meningitis were given Garlic extract orally and by injection. All eleven people recovered from this normally fatal disease.

In one study, ten AIDS patients were given Kyolic® liquid garlic extract for ten weeks while their normal natural killer cells and the helper/suppressor ratios in their immune systems were monitored. These readings were abnormal at the beginning of treatment, but by the end of the time period, six of seven patients had normal killer cell activity and four of seven patients had an improved killer/suppressor ratio. They also had a reduction in AIDS related symptoms including diarrhea, candidiasis, and genital herpes. This study was presented at the Fifth International Conference on AIDS in Montreal, Quebec, Canada in 1989,

In a 1973 experiment, nine people under the direction of pathologist Dr. Tariq Abdullah tested the effect of garlic on natural killer cells against tumor cells. Three groups of volunteers were instructed to take no garlic, large doses of raw garlic or aged garlic extract (Kyolic®). At the end of three weeks, blood samples were taken to determine how active each volunteer's natural killer cells were. The group taking raw garlic found their cells killed 139 percent more tumor cells than the group taking no garlic. The aged garlic extract group killed 159 percent more tumor cells than those of the control group.

Inasmuch as melanoma of the skin is so widespread throughout the United States, researchers at UCLA began using Aged Garlic Extract (Kyolic®) to treat this disease finding that it suppresses the growth of cancer cells. Dr. Hoon, says Aged Garlic Extract may be the perfect modality for the prevention of melanoma. Troubled by the rapid rise in the number of new bladder cancer cases each year (more than 50,000), West Virginia researchers led by Dr. Donald Lamm tried Kyolic® Aged Garlic Extract™. It reduced the tumor growth and according to Dr. Lamm, suggested that it will prove to be an extremely effective form of immunotherapy.

By now you should be convinced that garlic is basic to good health. It can protect against pollution, radiation and even stress, kill many forms of harmful microbes and strengthen a person's immunity. Garlic may also have great potential for retarding aging since it inhibits peroxidation, a natural process that is believed to be part of the cause of aging. The membranes of our cells in our bodies must be soft and flexible to keep us in optimum health. Peroxidation causes these cells to be stiff and inflexible and can lead to blood vessel damage and inhibition of food nutrients, all qualities that lead to premature aging and disease. The unique process of aging garlic inhibits this peroxidation process.

Garlic contains numerous minerals and vitamins including A, B1 and C, calcium, magnesium, iron, copper, zinc, selenium, potassium chloride, germanium (enhances the immune system), sulfur compounds and various amino acids. Garlic increases the body's ability to assimilate thiamine by enhancing its absorption. Thiamine is a key part of the enzyme which acts beneficially on liver cells. Garlic is also effective in the treatment of lead, mercury, cadmium and arsenic poisoning as its sulfur compounds bind these heavy metals facilitating excretion from the body. The major heavy metals such as cadmium, lead and mercury, weakens our resistance to cancer, destroy morale and taxes the immune system leading to other diseases. Kyolic® garlic has shown to increase the glutathione in the liver thus helping the body to rid itself of pesticides, chemicals and toxins. Garlic is not just for people approaching mid-life who want to avoid illness. It is beneficial for everyone and even if you don't like the taste of garlic, supplements can do the job equally as well or even better.

Whatever good garlic does, the effects do not depend upon its culinary demand, but socially scorned odor. "Allicin, the odoriferous chemical formed when a garlic clove is cut or bruised is not important at all," says Herbert Peirson, a doctor and consultant formerly with the U.S. National Cancer Institute. "Allicin is highly unstable and degrades instantly in processing, when exposed to heat, oxygen, light, proteins or changes in acidity," he explains. "It is not crucial to any of garlic's biological activities, which is good, because allicin is also toxic and can kill cells."

For years it was assumed that allicin was the effective component in garlic. But thanks to modern technology, we now know that this is not the case. The latest study by the Nobel Prize Chemistry Department of the University of California at Irvine, tested garlic products claiming to contain allicin and in October 1995 proved conclusively that these claims are false.

In 1990, Dr. Osamu Imada speaking at the First World Congress on Garlic indicated that allicin is one of the major harmful compounds in raw garlic and when garlic is aged, its toxicity is greatly reduced. Research is discovering that aged garlic extract is very therapeutic due to the fact that aging renders the garlic odorless and less irritating to the stomach. Aged garlic extract is standardized with S-allyl cysteine (SAC), a water-soluble sulfur-containing amino acid. The benefits of SAC have shown that it lowers serum cholesterol and triglycerides. Rather than degrading cholesterol, aged garlic extract appears to interfere with its synthesis better than other forms of garlic supplements. The aging of garlic enhances the activity of detoxifying anti-oxidant enzymes in our cells (SOD, Catalase, Glutathione) which triggers the immune system to ward off "the bad guys". Unless the cells in our body do the killing, we can never recover from the onslaught of diseases.

Presentations during the Designer Foods III-"Phytochemicals in Garlic, Soy & Licorice" symposium in 1994, presented findings from studies using Kyolic®, an aged garlic extract (AGE). In research in both in vitro systems and in animal brain models of Alzheimer's disease Kyolic® was shown to improve memories and to prevent neuronal degeneration and the onset of senile dementia. Dr. Gilles Fillion of the Pasteur Institute, Paris, France, reported that AGE also modulates serotonin receptor levels (often suppressed by stress, fatigue and depression) in directions indicative of new brain activity and enhanced brain nutrition. This is extremely good news for an aging population. AGE also has been shown to protect hemoglobin from too much oxidation, whereas raw garlic caused excess oxidation.

Aged garlic extract also offers liver protection, prevents cancer, reduces blood clot formation (in heart disease), combats viruses (including AIDS), fights infection, is an immune enhancer and has anti-free radical/anti-oxidative effects. Dr. John Milner of the Pennsylvania State University showed that AGE and it's major constituent S-allyl cysteine, greatly inhibited carcinogen-DNA adduct formation linked with lung and mammary cancer development in rats. AGE is the only standardized, stabilized and safe garlic extract containing lower amounts of the toxic fat-soluble and greater amounts of water-soluble constituents, than those that are currently available for clinical research purposes.

Studies have indicated that aged garlic extract helps combat infectious disease by strengthening the immune system. Research has determined that garlic actually attracts immune cells to the tissue. Aged Garlic Extract has been seen to inhibit Candida albicans growth, actually hastening the removal of these cells from the blood circulation, and is the only garlic that promotes the growth of friendly flora in our intestinal tract. In one study, aged garlic extract (AGE, Kyolic®), was even found to enhance the effectiveness of an influenza vaccine and when used alone was found to be as effective as the vaccine.

Since heart disease attacks more people during the mid-life and later years, it would be nice if we could give our bodies a better defense. Watching your diet and exercising have always been the rule, but many times that is not enough. Many heart attacks come from clogged arteries, meaning the blood sticks to the arterial walls eventually forming a blockage (arteriosclerosis). Normally smooth and non-sticking, the walls may become damaged because of environmental toxins or free radical damage, resulting in the blood sticking to those injured areas. These stuck cells then may release growth hormones and slowly get larger, picking up LDL (low density lipoprotein) cholesterol and becoming "fat". Eventually they will block blood flow to the heart.

Aged garlic extract can offer some protection to this process. Dr. Manfred Steins, Brown University and Dr. Robert I-San Lin, Ph.D., discovered that aged garlic extract and its active compounds are potent inhibitors of platelet adhesion. The only other substance to have this property is tocopherol, a form of Vitamin E. While aspirin may inhibit platelet aggregation, it cannot prevent platelet adhesion. Kyolic® Aged Garlic Extract™ has shown it does both and without side effects. Other studies have concluded that the active compounds of aged garlic extract (S-allyl cysteine and S-ally mercaptocysteine) inhibit the growth of cells which could eventually block the artery. Aged garlic extract also has been found to lower LDL cholesterol and suggested that it may also slow the body's cholesterol synthesis. Even though Kyolic® has had the majority of studies conducted on garlic's healthy benefits, Lictwer Pharmacy of Germany (makers of KWAI garlic) has had numerous studies performed on its cholesterol lowering effects.

Blood clots are another fear of aging people because they can break loose and go to places in the body that threaten life's functions. The body has the unique ability to determine when blood should clot and when it should stay fluid. Blood platelets normally are disc-like, however when the body requires clotting for wound repair, these same discs grow projecting arms which interlock to hold them together. This process is facilitated by and also dependent upon, a host of molecular and cellular activities. The danger comes when these clots travel in the bloodstream to places such as the heart or brain. Aged garlic extract and its active compounds are potent inhibitors of those substances that hold the clots together and thus is an effective blood thinner with virtually no side effects.

Free radical formation and resulting cell damage are found in arthritis, atherosclerosis, AIDS, cancer, premature aging, heart and other degenerative disease. Garlic contains thioallyl compounds (sulfur-containing) with those specifically found in aged garlic extract being potent free radical and oxidation fighters, and also protects lymphocytes from irradiation damage, as discovered in laboratory tests. Raw garlic powder and fresh garlic did not have these beneficial qualities.

Stress is a major contributor to illness and although we are told to meditate, take vacations, chill out or take calming drugs, stress still takes its toll. Aged garlic extract has proven to actually reduce the effects of stress by lowering levels of corticoid, a hormone, which is secreted by the body during stress, diminishing the effects stress has on our immune systems and levels of energy.

Aged garlic extract and its constituents S-allyl cysteine, allixin and diallyl sulfide, have been shown to inhibit breast cancer, bladder cancer, melanoma cells, skin, liver, lung and colon cancer. A prime carcinogen, aflatoxin B. (AFB), is linked with liver cancer and is produced by Aspergillus mold, contaminated peanuts, rice, cereal grains, corn, beans and sweet potatoes. AFB in its natural unmetabolized form is actually not damaging to the body. Once it enters the body, the enzyme system metabolizes and chemically reacts to it. Some of the products of this metabolism can bind to DNA and cause trouble. Our bodies do produce enzymes that can make AFB less toxic and excrete it from our body. Aged garlic can help by inhibiting the AFB from binding with the DNA and hastening the excretion of this toxin from the body thus giving us protection from this risk of liver cancer.

Analytical studies showed that all types of garlic supplements contain different beneficial ingredients and similar components, but in varied amounts. A prudent consumer should request that manufacturers provide data from toxicological testing as to the safety of their products. Aged garlic extract is the only commercially available garlic preparation that has been proven to be safe for long term supplementation. Studies continue to confirm benefits of garlic and further research may suggest how much we need to consume to maintain optimal functioning of the immune system as well as preventing and reversing atherosclerosis. The only commercial garlic present in AGE is Kyolic® with over a dozen patents (Heavy metal eliminant; Anti-virus agent) and patents pending (Immune enhancer; Antioxidant; Anti-stress agent; Friendly intestinal flora growth stimulant; Antitumor promoter, a fraction of AGE; Antioxidant, Polysulfide fraction of AGE; Liver-protective agent; Chemopreventive agent, S-Allyl cysteine; Antitumor agent, S-Ally cysteine; Antitumor promoter, Allixin, New steroid saponin in garlic; Antifungal agent.

Willem H. Khoe, MD, D.Ht, D.Ac., Ph.D confirms his usage of an aged garlic extract, Kyolic® and we reprint* his list of indications below:

Hair Growth	6-8 capsules/day can prevent hair from falling out. Results also showed thicker hair and a darker color.
Nose	Liquid Kyolic® Mixed in a vaporizer, helps free nasal passages.
Ears	3-4 drops on a "Q-tip" can help ear infections and fungus of the ear canal.
Throat	Diluted in water can be an effective gargle for throat soreness, tonsillitis and laryngitis.
Heart disease	4 capsules/day as preventative.
Arthritis	4-6 capsules/day with a diet free of simple sugars has relieved many

	patients of pain depending on condition.
Gastritis	If there is no serious cause, even ulcer and gastritis can be helped by adding Kyolic® and Kyo-Dophilus® after each meal.
Influenza	At the first sign of flu take 4 capsules 3x/day for two days.
Colitis	Both acute and chronic have been relieved with a combination of Kyolic® and Kyo-Dophilus®.
Athletes foot	Apply liquid Kyolic® to affected area with swab.
Constipation	5 capsules of Kyolic® or 1 tsp of the liquid and 2 Kyo-Dophilus® after each meal.
Diabetes	By using 4 capsules a day, one can decrease the insulin intake.
Worms	Many a child has been relieved from pinworms in just a few days. Insert 1 capsule into the rectum of the child at bedtime.

*Excerpted from The Khoe Newsletter

As important as garlic may be, it should never be a substitute for the foundation of good health which is pure air, water, food, fiber, exercise and a positive outlook. Garlic is the best example that food can be medicine.

SKIN..

Young fresh skin is no longer an illusion. From time immemorial beauty and a youthful appearance have moved hearts. Today skin care, and particularly facial care, is an important element of the conscious experience of well being, personality, attractiveness, and individuality. In this chapter, we will discuss how to dramatically slow down, prevent and eliminate aging of the skin.

Beautiful skin is more than 'skin deep'. The skin is the largest organ of nourishment and elimination, with the acid mantle, or covering of the skin, inhibiting the growth of disease causing bacteria. Skin problems are one of the surest signs of poor nutrition and improved nutrition is quickly mirrored by skin health. Some of the causes of skin problems are emotional stress, poor diet of refined foods and sugar, too many saturated fats, caffeine overload, food allergies, liver malfunction, poor digestion and assimilation, irritating cosmetics, essential fatty acid depletion, synthetic fiber clothing, PMS and menopausal changes.

Beginning at the age of thirty, there is a reduction of elastin and collagen production in the connective tissue where the elastic and collagen fibers are found. The skin enzyme "elastase" attacks the elastic fibers and destroys the elastic, therefore your skin loses its tone. The contour of your skin, wrinkles and lines are determined by many factors including moisture and the relative health of collagen. Aging of the skin occurs when collagen becomes hard and crosslinked with neighboring collagen fibers. The cause of the crosslinking is oxidation, or free-radical formation. Free radicals attack cell membranes, genetic cell material and the collagen and elastin proteins causing wrinkles, sagging contours, sallow complexion and skin cancer. Some of the causes of free radical damage are smog and environment pollutants, too much sunlight (UVA and UVB), stress, poor diet, liver exhaustion, and skin dehydration caused by estrogen depletion.

Through the ages, women used wine on their face and body to smooth their skin. The tartaric acid in the wine sloughed off old dead skin! Cleopatra used to bathe in milk, as the lactic acid helped to give her beautiful skin. History has proven natural formulas work and since what ever goes on our skin, eventually finds its way into our body, a great many cosmetic formulas now take a natural approach to skin care products.

These 'natural' cosmetics may include Alpha Hydroxy Acids or AHA's as they are called. AHA is the family name for a number of acids, such as, glycolic acids (sugar cane); citric acid (citrus fruit); lactic acid (sour milk), malic acid (apples) and tartaric acid (aged wine). In the Beta range an example would be salicylic acid (meadowsweet).

The most popular of these relatives is glycolic acid due to it's small molecular weight so it can penetrate many layers of the skin. These acids (which need to be from natural sources only) have been found to soften rough skin, reduce wrinkles, lighten age spots (actinic keratosis), increase moisture retention, speed up cellular exfoliation, balance skin pH and even skin discoloration's. By putting the full range of AHA's and BHA's together a more thorough result can be achieved. For example, Beta acid (salicylic acid) is an antiseptic which can control bacteria from causing certain skin problems. It is also an anti-aging and a pain reducer and provides preservative abilities due to it's anti-fungal nature.

The newly discovered algae extract, aosain, protects and strengthens the connective tissue and counteracts the loss of elasticity in the skin. Aosain is obtained from the Aosa Algae, which is so elastic it endures the stormy seas of

Brittany without being smashed on the rocks. This protective mechanism of the algae extract when transported into the deeper layers of the epidermis, retards the damaging effects of the elastase enzyme and so counteracts the natural reduction of elastin. Active almond protein also can stimulate the production of collagen and elastin to prevent loss and firm tone. Vitamin A and E stimulate cell regeneration and support skin regeneration. Vitamin E can also protect against free radical damage.

The skin's moisture content begins to diminish early in life. After age 30, up to 25 percent is lost and by age 40, as much as 50 percent is lost. Wrinkles and sagging skin are evidence of skin dehydration. A billion dollar industry has developed to provide products that will keep moisture in skin as it ages. Unfortunately, most of these creams, lotions, etc. are plastered on the skin to try and keep moisture in. If the skin is moisture deficient, wouldn't it be smarter to add moisture as well as try to retain moisture?

Humectants are what causes a cactus to draw moisture out of the desert air, and our bodies also produce their own humectants, specifically, NaPCA. This natural moisturizer can be produced synthetically in a laboratory. Both types are derived from glutamic acid, one of the non-essential amino acids occurring in humans. NaPCA, present on our skin surface, may be a direct cause of glowing natural beauty, while its decline brings on the deep furrows and inelasticity of age. The skin has the ability to hold moisture and as the level of NaPCA decreases with age, the moisture content of the skin begins to drop as well. NaPCA is a water soluble substance, light enough for any skin to use and available commercially as a body spray and within skin care products.

Herbs, when combined with crystalloid trace minerals (electrolytes) can be a nourishing complement in a moisturizing skin spray. These nutrients penetrate to the deepest layers of the skin, carrying oxygen molecules across the cell wall. Electrolytes enhance tissue oxygenation aiding the reduction of free radical formation, and can be a major factor in slowing down our skin's aging process! Crystalloid trace minerals, which give 100 percent solubility, penetrate the epidermal barrier, rejuvenating cell function of the deepest layer where skin is made. The minerals also capture and stabilize free-radicals before they damage and wrinkle skin. Wheat germ protein, macadamia nut oil and moisture-retaining hyaluronic acid can smooth fine lines caused by dry skin.

Combinations of various healing herbs such as Aloe vera, Horsetail (silica), Chamomile, Comfrey, and Burdock Root, when bonded with electrolytes, readily enters the bloodstream and penetrates the cells of the body. This initiates a healing response that benefits the entire organism, similar to a full symphony orchestra coming into play. Electrolytes are a trans-dermal nutrient healer and an important aid to skin rejuvenation. Good skin hydration is one of the most important aspects of attaining and maintaining youthful skin.

Oils have long been known to feed the skin, but not all oils can do the job. Squalane is produced by our bodies in a very small amount (3 to 5 percent). However most people do not synthesize enough of this vital oil which leads to rough, dry aging skin. The oil is so fine it is absorbed deep into the skin very quickly and helps to discourage the growth of bacteria that can block healthy cell development. At the same time it helps protect it from the harmful effects of sun, winter cold, smoke and pollution. The purest form of squalane is found in shark liver oil (from the deep oceans) and is 99.9 percent pure. Olive and avocado oil which are also found in skin products, are around 96 percent pure.

Stay away from petroleum based oils, such as mineral oil. Petroleum products can not be absorbed by skin, are not compatible with, and are foreign to cellular structure. Active substances are blocked by petroleum products so they cannot be absorbed. They also obstruct pore/follicle orifices which can cause clogged pores, blocking normal perspiration and hair growth. Read labels on your cosmetics and make sure they do not contain a petroleum oil (many commercial lipsticks, skin softeners and lip balms are petroleum based). Remember, you are ingesting this petroleum through the skin and lips...would you eat motor oil?

Keeping your immune system in tip top shape will result in a healthy, young outer appearance. In addition to nutrients mentioned in other chapters, green foods and enzymes, taken internally play a large part in the health of your skin. Seaweed has a composition so close to human plasma that it can help balance the cells of the body. Seaweed, kelp, and red marine algae, help nourish and hydrate aging skin when used both topically and internally. Calcium and magnesium in seaweed drain fluid out of tissues, helping to fight water retention and reduce cellulite. Red marine algae helps the cells to grow rapidly, improve skin firmness and elasticity, and result in smoother, less lined skin. Using these natural plants from the water, can quickly control or eliminate fingernail fungus, athlete's foot or other fungal infections of the skin.

Enzymes taken internally are an important part of cellular rejuvenation. Topically, they can help the skin directly, especially green papaya, which has the ability to dissolve dead damaged skin cells, while leaving healthy cells intact. Green papaya is found to contain the highest degree of enzyme complex. It is a natural complement to products containing glycolic acid and also contains more vitamin A,C, and E than any other natural product. Green papaya also has an abundance of B factors and the concentrate contains pure, raw honey, known for its ability to soften the surface of the skin.

The pH of the skin mantle normally ranges from 4.5 to 5.5 and most often referred to as 5.5. Many products would not be as effective if they had a reading of 5.5. For example, a cleanser formulated with a pH of 7, which is neutral, will cleanse the skin better than a pH of 5.5 (acid). A moisturizer that is slightly alkaline will have a softening effect, making it easier for the skin to absorb the beneficial ingredients in the moisturizer. Products that are formulated for skin with an acne condition are more acidic to help fight germs. The lower the pH number, the more acidic, and the higher the number, the more alkaline.

Men's skin is different from women's and must be treated slightly different. Men have thicker skin and this means more oil glands with natural lubrication that delays facial lines and wrinkles caused by dry skin. Because of this type of skin, men develop fewer, but more deeply etched lines. Shaving becomes man's daily exfoliating ritual and encourages cell renewal similar to women's facial scrubs, therefore any exfoliants used can be less abrasive. To prevent drying the skin, men should not use aerosol shaving foams which are no more than drying soaps, filled with air. Try using all natural facial cleansers as shaving lather, as well as non-alcoholic after shaves (non drying) with soothing ingredients such as aloe. Men can also use an NaPCA and herbal mineral (electrolyte) spray to add moisture back into the skin.

The following information will show both women and men how to prevent and correct skin problems due to aging.

PROBLEM: Adult Acne

PREVENTION: Crystalloid Trace Minerals; Vitamin A (fish liver oil); E.F.A. (omega 3 and 6); Aloe, Burdock Root, Chamomile, Comfrey, and Horsetail (silica) blended with Electrolytes. Use natural products without petroleum ingredients which dry, irritate the skin and can interfere with normal perspiration and skin activity. Use a good natural scrub 3-4 times a week that contains jojoba esters. Avoid products with apricot pits, walnut shells or almond seeds which are abrasive and can actually cut and irritate the skin.

ELIMINATION: Use products that are cold processed (not heated) to maintain their natural nutrients and have stabilized oxygen to oxygenate the skin. They may contain homepathics which balance and nourish the skin, jojoba or sunflower oils, and sea alginate (which contains natural antioxidants and nutrients). Take kelp micronutrients which is rich in vitamin and minerals for good skin and hair. Drink 6-8 glasses per day, of purified water with liquid crystalloid minerals added. Get the appropriate amount of sleep, and learn to live an stress-free way of life.

PROBLEM: Age Spots

PREVENTION: Use a daily regimen of glycolic acids along with green papaya and a good moisturizer to protect the skin. Internally, add to your drinking water, crystalloid trace minerals, especially zinc and selenium, in a electrolyte form, Also take Vitamin A (fish liver oil), Vitamin C and Nutritional Yeast to remove top layers of skin and to aid cellular rejuvenation. Calcium and magnesium (in equal amounts) helps to restore, firm and tone, the skin and improve circulation.

ELIMINATION: Use products with alpha and beta hydroxies, to improve and eliminate skin discoloration, and improve circulation. Add products with or orally take stabilized oxygen to help other ingredients work better (herbs blended with electrolytes). Use a masque that contains a apple cider vinegar containing natural acids that can fade melatonin spots. Herbal treatments are listed in the chapter on herbs, flowers and homeopathics.

PROBLEM: Cellulite
PREVENTION: Much cellulite is developed because of heredity precursors, although joggers have been known to lose their long term cellulite after following a continuous exercise program. Exercise and muscle toning is helpful in reducing the effects of cellulite.
ELIMINATION: Cellulite may be reduced through exercise and using herbs such as Ehinacea, Rosemary, Camphor, Butcherbroom and Horsetail (silica) to activate and firm the skin. Applications of vegetable oils such as jojoba, macadamia nut, babassu and squalane help to smooth the skin. Skin massage with a loofa or skin brush helps to break up the cellulite.

PROBLEM: Dark Circles/Eye Bags
PREVENTION: Use mineral based eye gel with silicea proline and Calc. Flour. (homeopathic) to firm skin connective tissues, along with an herbal electrolyte skin spray. Products with homeopathic oxygenating complex and stabilized oxygen, will oxygenate the area improving circulation and flushing toxins helping to eliminate dark circles as well as improving circulation. Drinking Japanese green tea or using products with Japanese green tea are good because the high tannin content helps tone the skin and eliminate toxins. Cleansing the liver with milk thistle

and trace minerals (crystalloid form) will help to prevent the dark circles

ELIMINATION: Use of a quality masque around the sinus area can improve circulation and open sinus areas which are clogged and cause puffy eyes. Skin care products with stabilized oxygen which is anti-bacterial and anti-viral, bring more oxygen to the area improving circulation and helps minor infections which can cause puffiness or discoloration. Buy a good clay and make a masque to draw out facial toxins. Drinking 6-8 glasses of purified water (with electrolytes) flushes the liver improving bladder and kidney function and helps them increase their ability to flush out toxins from the system. Honey and vinegar taken once a day improve body function and help improve dark circles/eye bags.

PROBLEM: Dry skin
PREVENTION: same as adult acne
ELIMINATION: Use a moisturizer without petroleum products which dry and irritate the skin. Spray the skin with products containing NaPCA, herbs and minerals. Taking vitamin A (fish liver oil) and vitamin E which helps to regulate sebaceous glands. Green papaya, and seaweed source (kelp or Red marine algae) puts the important trace minerals back into the cells. Use alpha and beta hydroxies to normalize moisture retention., and squalane to replenish the oils in the skin.

PROBLEM: Oily skin
PREVENTION: same as adult acne
ELIMINATION: Use products with alpha and beta hydroxies to normalize oil secretion and reduce enlarged pores. Apply a masque (clay) to deep cleanse with the full range of minerals and trace minerals to regulate the glands.

Use a product containing balsam peru which has been used to heal skin conditions and is excellent for acne and traumatized skin. Take homeopathic Nat. Mur. to balance oil secretion in the body and add extra (riboflavin) vitamin B2.

PROBLEM: Sallow color
PREVENTION: Same as age spots. Use a jojoba oil.
ELIMINATION: Same as age spots. Take homeopathic iron phosphate to bring oxygen to the system and improve skin color and health.

PROBLEM: Wrinkles
PREVENTION: As we age, the dead skin cells do not slough off as quickly, so it is important to speed up process with the use of products containing alpha and beta hydroxies, to aid in cell rejuvenation keep skin fresh and soft, clean pores, remove dead skin, improve cell circulation, and retain moisture. Use an all natural lotion/moisturizer with sea alginate which has natural oxygenators and form a protective barrier to lock in moisture which tends to leave older skin more quickly. Spray skin with solution containing NaPCA. Use products with hybrid sunflower oil and/or jojoba oils which are closest to the skin pH and sebum quality. Take trace minerals (crystalloid), calcium and magnesium which will fight free radicals, improve skin health and tone, assist circulation, and aid toxin removal. Use a loofah sponge in circular motion.
ELIMINATION: Use products with homeopathic silicea, proline, and Calc. Fluor. to firm skin connective tissues and Kali. Phos. to strengthen collagen and elastin tissues. Use products with alpha and beta hydroxies and green papaya to aid cell rejuvenation, clean and open pores, slough off

dead skin, improve cell circulation, aid moisture retention and reduce fine lines and wrinkles. Take vitamin A (fish liver oil), B complex, C, and E, because antioxidants help cellular growth. Take trace minerals (crystalloid form), and calcium with magnesium, in equal amounts. Adding flaxseed (omega 3 and 6) to your diet helps to reduce wrinkles and fine lines. Use products with or orally take stabilized oxygen to help other ingredients work better.

PROBLEM: Wrinkled hands
PREVENTION: Since skin on the hands age faster than the rest of the body, it is important to use a masque that conditions and nourishes. Use products with alpha and beta hydroxies to prevent wrinkles by increasing cell regeneration, improve and eliminate skin discoloration and improve circulation. Use green papaya enzyme to aid cell rejuvenation, squalane to rebuild skin tone and taking vitamin A (fish liver oil) and vitamin E to help maintain the elasticity of the skin.

Remember, your skin is only a reflection of your blood stream and your blood stream a reflection of your digestive tract. The secret of staying young, is truly from within.

SIGNS OF AGING...

Fifty is a milestone for both men and women because their bodily changes are becoming obvious, not normally for the better. Aches, pains and threat of debilitating disease become a closer reality. It is our belief that both men and women are affected by hormonal changes and although men don't get hot flashes, they can be affected by the other conditions described in this chapter.

Osteoporosis happens when the body fails to utilize calcium which leeches out of the bone. It affects women and men as well, most noticeably by the reduction of height in older individuals. Also in both men and women, jawbones shrink causing a sagging or jowly face.

The normal time for rebuilding of solid bone is ten to twelve years and for the spongy bone, two to three years with five to ten percent of our bone being replaced by this process each year. As we age, more bone is broken down than is created. Drug therapies currently given to prevent blood vessels from breaking down the bone, may actually produce an overabundance of new bone that competes for space with the old bone. This bone disparity creates more risk of fracture.

There are better ways to prevent bone loss. If we have built a good quantity of bone mass during our younger years, our bone loss will be less. therefore it is important to start being concerned about osteoporosis well before you reach fifty. Taking royal jelly can help to accelerate the formation of bone tissue, and by keeping a balanced pH as discussed in an earlier chapter, you can create an essential condition for bone making. Most people think that by just adding a calcium supplement you will build up your defense against osteoporosis. This is not the case. Magnesium must be taken as well because it is a carrier for the calcium on its trip to the bone. If too much calcium is taken, it will actually cause a magnesium deficiency in the body resulting in nervousness, fatigue, heart palpitations and depression. Excess calcium also can work to prevent this calcium from getting into the bones at all.

It is important to take calcium and magnesium in a 1:1 ration. Do not eat quantities of dairy (better to substitute with rice or almond milk products), without supplementing your diet with magnesium rich foods such as kale, seeds, nuts, barley and wheatgrass and dark green vegetables. Avoid sugar, sodas containing phosphoric acid and the diuretic Lasix as they all contribute to leeching calcium from the body. During and after menopause the body's ability to hold on to calcium declines, and bone-calcium loss can be intense for as long as ten years after menopause. Osteoporosis, is a repercussion of imbalance. The equilibrium of specific minerals in the blood, including calcium, is critical, and the body has special mechanisms to ensure their constancy. Calcium's availability fluctuates all the time, so the bones act as a "bank" which the body can draw on if dietary calcium is low, or return calcium to. when the absorption is high. Although this system can be disrupted by dieting and inadequate nutrition, excesses of certain non-foods and processed foods, unremitting stress, and long-term use of certain drugs, it is generally not until menopause that the process of bone loss becomes accelerated to a critical point.

Trace minerals or electrolytes are involved in the health of the glands and the production of the hormones that control calcium's use in the body. All the body's functions are sensitive to changes in mineral balance. For example, if the body is out of homeostasis, calcium deficiency will occur, no matter how high the calcium intake. A high intake of calcium may disrupt the body's levels of zinc, iron and manganese and these minerals also influence calcium's absorption. In order to absorb and use calcium the body needs vitamin D, magnesium and trace minerals including copper. Too much vitamin A, E or potassium will upset calcium metabolism and decrease its availability.

When our bodies are low in calcium, they can borrow from reserves in the bones. Magnesium is also stored in the bones, which won't give up as much of it as calcium. Instead our bodies take magnesium from muscles. Without enough magnesium in muscles to counterbalance the stimulating effect of calcium, they stiffen up or contract at will resulting in cramps, irritability, twitching or tremors.

Boron is a naturally occurring trace mineral that should be part of any calcium/magnesium supplement. It decreases the urinary excretion of calcium and magnesium and increases blood levels of estrogen, vitamin D and other hormones. Boron, found mainly in fruit, raises serum estrogen levels in post menopausal women thereby reducing calcium and magnesium loss. Silica influences the uptake of calcium in the bones and can be transmuted to calcium in the body. Silica also has the wonderful advantage (to women especially), of strengthening nails and causing them to grow. Vitamin D has shown to reduce the incidence of hip fractures in post-menopausal women. In a study at Tufts University, women who took 400 I.U. of vitamin D daily has less bone loss during the winter months (lack of adequate sunlight), than women who took a placebo.

Exercise influences bone density and trace minerals aid the absorption of nutrients (100 percent), together they make a winning team of preventing osteoporosis. In our chapter on fitness we give several bone building exercises. Stay away from sugar, as it inhibits calcium absorption, alters insulin metabolism which affects calcium metabolism, and loss of vitamin B6 levels which upset magnesium...but worst of all, it robs the body of trace minerals so rapidly and thoroughly that it upsets every physical process and increases the long-term risk of osteoporosis.

Estrogen is important in carrying calcium and magnesium from the bloodstream to the bones, therefore women are more susceptible to osteoporosis when their estrogen levels drop during menopause. Adding estrogen alone may not prevent the acceleration of bone loss. Progesterone stimulates bone formation and during menopause, adding back natural progesterone (described below), combined with estrogen helps restore this hormone imbalance.

It is also essential that you supplement your diet with enzymes to guard against osteoporosis. The protease enzyme is important in calcium metabolism and plant enzymes aid proper digestion necessary for the nutrient extraction needed for healthy bones. When shopping for enzymes make sure they say 'plant source' on the bottle or you will not be getting the full complement of enzymes.

Hot flashes are not really fever-like temperature rises, although try telling that to most women who are in the midst of taking off their sweaters...again! They occur when there are changes in the diameter of the blood vessels near the skin surface making only the skin temperature rise. When levels of adrenaline and cortisone are increased in the body, such as during darkness, hot flashes result. Low sodium can also cause an increase in adrenaline, so taking a crystalloid trace mineral solution, will help. Hot flashes can be triggered by dietary habits, alcohol, tobacco, coffee, spicy foods and eating large meals.

Pantothenic Acid is useful to help stress and is necessary for adrenal function; therefore if hot flashes persist try adding this supplement to your diet. Good news for women who carry a little extra fat, comes from the menopausal practitioners. Because an adrenal hormone can be converted to estrogen and stored in body fat, it seems that thin women seem to suffer more during menopause than those that are heavier. Don't take this as an excuse to gorge yourself because obese women are high risk for uterine and breast cancer due to too much estrogen production. Natural progesterone supplementation, from the organic wild yam, can balance this condition. In a study of 100 postmenopausal women who were experiencing signs of osteoporosis, the wild yam progesterone cream resulted in a 10% increase in bone density during the first six months of treatment and an annual increase of 3-5% in most of the women.

The production of progesterone from cholesterol is dependent on adequate thyroid function plus vitamin A (fish oil source is best) and certain enzymes. Adding natural progesterone along with vitamin A and enzymes may help to control night sweats. Using estrogen alone to diminish hot flashes is like using a drug. It keeps the body in a continuous state of excitation causing increased levels of adrenaline. It works because a hot flash occurs when adrenal levels are in a relaxed state, after an increase. Like keeping yourself awake with coffee, estrogen keeps you in an "up" state so the adrenaline levels never go down. This may prevent hot flashes, but can also create numerous side effects.

Vitamin E (combined with vitamin C as a carrier) can reduce hot flashes and also improve circulation, as well as help prevent varicose veins and blood clots. Recommended dosages should come from a physician or a naturopathic doctor, as overdoses may cause some side effects especially in diabetics or people taking blood thinners or high blood pressure medicine.

Evening primrose oil, a source of the essential fatty acid GLA (gamma-linolenic acid), is necessary for hormone production and has been successful at reducing the effects of hot flashes. Omega 3 and Omega 6 fatty acids, found in certain oils or ground flax seed, are beneficial in reducing hot flashes. Herbal remedies include Dong quai, Ginseng, Hawthorn berries, Black cohosh, Wild Yam root, Chaste Tree berry and Licorice root. These herbs are good for all around menopausal symptom relief. Homeopathic remedies include Lachesis and Pulsatilla.

Estrogen and progesterone supplementation is not fully understood by menopausal people who may be abusing their bodies with these creams and pills. When estrogen and progesterone levels decrease, the slack is picked up by the adrenal glands. If our bodies are stressed, our adrenals become exhausted and are unable to produce the needed hormones. This is important for men as well as women.

Estrogen may increase the growth of existing cancers, especially when it is taken in continuous small doses, unless it balanced by progesterone. It can create other side effects as well such as increased risk of pituitary cancers, liver dysfunction, gall bladder attacks, water retention, and weight gain. Estrogen replacement therapy must always include a healthy ratio of progesterone to estrogen of ten to one.

You may be getting excess estrogen without even taking a supplement as many chemicals like chlorine, pesticides and PCBs (petroleum byproducts) mimic estrogen in the body. Excess estrogen is also associated with heart problems, stroke and hypoxia (lack of oxygen). Women who have ratios of less than five progesterone to one estrogen, are prone to cyclic seizures, excessive bleeding, fibrocystic breast disease, and ovarian cysts. It also promotes thyroid deficiencies because it inhibits thyroid secretion, resulting in symptoms such as headaches, frequent infections, insomnia, fatigue, depression, constipation, cancer and squamous metaplasia in prostate

100

cells, a precancerous condition, to name a few.

The ovaries aren't the only producers of estrogen. Androgens (specifically androstenedione, an adrenal hormone) can be converted to estrogen in both men and women. Men's estrogen level production goes up as their testosterone levels decrease. In women, after menopause, the conversion of androgens and progesterone to estrogen can occur if thyroid function is inadequate. Adrenal stimulants include sugar and caffeine and can contribute to progesterone deficiencies. Men can experience an over estrogen condition whereby they develop higher voices and breast fat as they age.

Since the key to producing adrenal gland hormones is progesterone, when it's lacking, the body produces the androstenedione, which has a masculinizing effect on women. It also can contribute to thinning hair in men. Natural progesterone is not the same as synthetic progestins which have side effects such as depression, acne, and weight gain. Synthetic progestins may be carcinogenic and inhibit the production of your own natural progesterone. Natural progesterone actually stimulates its own synthesis in the body. Semi-synthetic progesterone (Progesterone U.S.P.) extracted from wild yams, may not include some of the plant's natural enzymes, peptides or other phytosterols having been destroyed in the extraction process. These are important phytochemicals the body needs to nurture itself. They may be quite effective in reducing menopausal symptoms at the onset, but they will mean trouble down the road. Even a small dosage of 25mg/day can block pathways in the endocrine system, raising cholesterol levels and requiring stronger and stronger dosages to work as it will eventually desensitize receptor sites.

Progesterone replacement is best done naturally with products containing the <u>organic</u> wild yam which is nearly identical to what the body produces. The method of extraction must be one that leaves all the nutrients in tact. James Jamieson, pharmacologist, is currently working with over 110 species of wild yams. He says, " You have to be careful not to disturb the delicate synergism and balance as each phytogen, peptide, enzyme, co-enzyme and other co-factors because they all have different and remarkable actions and activities in the body". Synthetic, semi-synthetic and many "natural" progesterones do not respect mother nature's wisdom and will provide only that substance that gets immediate results. Also many wild yam creams or tinctures can be hazardous to your health because they contain pesticides, whose residue will mimic pseudoestrogens and definitely destroy the endocrine balance. Be sure that your wild yam supplement of choice is organic and has all its natural nutrients in tact.

Baldness is some men's main concern with aging. It is a sure symbol that they are getting old. Balding is not necessarily genetic or permanent and sometimes may be related to oxygen starvation of the cells in the scalp. It can be precipitated by the over consumption of certain dietary fats, such as hydrogenated margarine and unfermented soybean products.

In a test it was found that sheep that ate a diet of raw soybean plants experienced a loss of hair. It seems the unfermented soybean has a biochemical component, phyto-hemagglutinin, that may act as a glue in the blood contributing to hair loss. Fat laden blood goes directly to the head where the soy oil causes the red blood cells to stick together and plug the blood capillaries. This will reduce the oxygen to the scalp and the hair follicles, and literally smothers the scalp. Gray hair can be caused by this condition and also to vitamin deficiencies. De-toxing and rebuilding the immune system may clear out these clogged areas and provide a healthy environment for new hair growth, but you should avoid hydrogenated oils and unfermented soy products to guard against baldness. For other treatments refer to the chapter, *Herbs, Flowers, Bees and Homeopathics.*

Degenerative arthritis is considered by some to be an inevitable part of aging. It is caused by a toxic body trying to rid itself of waste. When salts combine with other wastes they precipitate out of the blood and lymph fluids forming abrasive deposits. These end up in the joints causing bursitis and arthritis which may also be caused or aggravated by the demineralization of the bones, which is leeched out to service our mineral deficient bodies.

Since most of our foods and water are lacking minerals, it is necessary to replace them with a crystalloid electrolyte supplement. This disease may be caused by cortisone drugs which, if taken over a long period of time, tend to affect the solidity of bone. In order to avoid an arthritic condition, it is very important to maintain a toxic free lifestyle thereby freeing the body from its arduous task of removing these toxins.

In the chapter, *Essential Fatty Acids*, we discussed the use of GLA (Gamma Linolenic Acid) from Borage, Evening Primrose & Black Currant Oils. Applications of these oils as it applies to rheumatoid arthritis has shown to be effective in reducing inflammation and joint tenderness. All GLA oils have the ability to effect these results although larger dosages are required of Evening Primrose and Black Currant Oils than Borage Oil.

Cleansing and supporting the immune system will help reduce the effects of arthritis in the long run, but for relatively immediate relief drink black cherry juice (best to use the concentrate diluted in water or juice), and use royal jelly (from worker bees). Herbal remedies include those that incorporate; Nettles, Red Clover, compounded Juniper berry, compounded Yucca/Burdock, Garlic, seaweed and nutritional yeast are great alternatives to a pain pill, when taken as a regular supplement. (See chapter, *Herbs, Flowers, Bees and Homeopathics*) Cayenne pepper capsules can bring blood to the joints and muscles to keep them warm and flexible, especially if you are living a sedentary lifestyle.

Memory loss. The brain's remarkable ability to perceive and perform, remember and learn, is severely challenged by today's social and physical environment. These factors accelerate the decline in nerve cell activity that normally occurs with age. Phosphatidyl Serine (PS) is a phospholipid which forms an essential part in every human cell, but it is particularly concentrated in the membranes of nerve cells. Unlike other cells in the body, nerve cells do not reproduce. Instead, they repair and rebuild themselves, using proteins called Nerve Growth Factor (NGF). PS enhances the synthesis and reception of NGF and support brain functions that tend to diminish with age. PS also may be related to the body's response to stress, as taking a PS supplement appears to produce fewer stress hormones in response to exercise-induced stress. PS may have the potential to minimize a common problem in today's world, stress induced memory lapse.

HERBS, FLOWERS, BEES AND HOMEOPATHICS

Since the days of the Old Testament, humans have been tapping the enormous healing power of plants. Multi-billion dollar drug companies have not ignored the importance of herbs, with one-third of all prescription drugs sold in the United States being herbal extracts. Vincristine, a potent anti-cancer drug for childhood leukemia is made from the periwinkle plant and Digitalis, a common heart medicine is made from the foxglove plant. Folk remedies have included penicillin from moldy bread, aspirin naturally occurring in white willow and even quinine used for malaria, found in the Cinchona bark of the rain forests.

For thousands of years, the leaves of the ginkgo tree have been recognized for their benefits as a geriatric remedy. The most interesting and important relate to vascular disease, brain function, impotency, asthma and inflammation. By improving circulation, Ginkgo is a powerful treatment for restoring and boosting memory. A recent study published in a major scientific journal shows that an extract of this ancient botanical, successfully restored erections to impotent men.

Garlic is a potent healer and traditional natural remedy and if it were not a food, would take ten years of scientific research and millions of dollars to fully test this "wonder drug" before it could attain Food and Drug Administration approval. In Sweden, blueberry extract and its drug name Pecarin, is used in the treatment of diarrhea. Cranberries have long been known to alleviate urinary tract infections, but unfortunately this and other natural remedies cannot be patented and therefore has no monetary value to drug companies.

Herbs are concentrated foods, whole essences, with the ability to address both the symptoms and causes of a problem. They are nutritional foundation nutrients, working through the glands, nourishing the body's deepest basic elements. Balance is the key to using herbal nutrients for healing with each person reacting differently. Herbs work better in combination than they do alone and results from herbs may not be immediate. A rule of thumb says one month of healing for every year of the illness. People wishing to find alternatives to drugs have investigated herbs, foods as well as homeopathic, biochemical and flower remedies. Chinese herbs have been used in healing for over 4,000 years. Balancing body, mind and spirit is the core of Traditional Chinese Medicine which combines the healing power of plants with the energy they release for specific conditions (similar to homeopathics). They will be indicated with a * in the following remedy section.

Bees have been helping people for centuries. They collect pollen from flowers and deposit it in the honeycomb cell where it is concentrated, and becomes a high source of nutrients. RNA and DNA are found in abundant quantities in bee pollen as well as rutin, which strengthens capillaries. It has been suggested that it can control the runaway growth of cancer cells, reduce alcohol craving, increase IQ and the powers of concentration. High in lecithin, bee pollen also contributes to the increase in brain function. Taken before and during allergy season, it has been effective in preventing the onset of symptoms. When purchasing bee pollen products, research their drying process. Heating or microwaving, a popular method, kills beneficial organisms, therefore natural drying and/or freezing is best.

Another bee 'product' is royal jelly, the white, milky substance produce in the glands of worker honeybees to feed the queen and help her grow 40-60% larger than the other bees. Royal jelly contains all of the B-complex vitamins, A,C,D, and E, minerals, enzymes, hormones, eighteen amino acids as well as antibacterial and antibiotic components. It is known to aid asthma, liver disease, pancreatitis, insomnia, stomach ulcers, kidney disease, bone fractures and skin disorders. It aids the immune system and produces an age-retarding, longevity enhancing effect.

Propolis is the bees' natural defense against bacteria, fungi and viruses. It can act against viruses which current antibiotics do not, by preventing them from reproducing. Since antibiotics from flavonoids, such as propolis, possess a cellular structure similar to the human body, they may be much more effective than existing antibiotics such as penicillin and streptomycin. Propolis also is an antioxidant free-radical scavenger and can stimulate the body's own immune system to resist disease. According to John Diamon, M.D., president of the International Academy of Preventive Medicine, propolis may be the most strengthening to the thymus, of all the natural supplements he tested. It can be used topically for healing wounds and infections, treating ulcers, controlling cancer and for sore throats, coughs, colds, sinusitus and tonsillitis.

And of course, for healing bee products we can't forget to mention honey. If it is unprocessed and made in an organic environment, it can be used topically as a dressing agent in surgical infections, burns and wound infections, and is an old folk remedy for stomach upset, sore throats and as a more healthful sugar substitute

Homeopathic remedies treat illness by stimulation of the body's own healing response. They are prepared from natural substances; plant, mineral and animal. Homeopathic treatment operates under the premise that the same natural substances that cause a set of symptoms if given to a healthy individual in large quantities, can also stimulate a sick individual to get better if given in tiny amounts. Every disease which afflicts the human race indicates a lack of some inorganic constituent of the body, and biochemic supplements given in small quantities helps to restore that which is missing. Flower remedies tend to work on the emotional level, from which many of our ailments originate. Since illness can be influenced positively or negatively by a person's mental state, flower remedies may head sickness off at the pass! There are numerous books that describe these alternative methods in detail, so we won't re-invent the wheel, but just to give you quick reference, we have listed some of the more common methods for treatment of illness that people tend to develop as they age.

Remedies excerpted from the following sources:
Healing Nutrients by Dr. P. Quillan; The Biochemic Handbook by J.B. Chapman, MD and Edward L. Perry, MD; Traditional Home & Herbal Remedies by Jan De Vries, Naturopathic Handbook of Herbal Formulas, information on flower remedies supplied by Mighty Oak, homeopathic remedies supplied by Bioforce and Homeopathic Works, herbal suggestions by Bioforce and herbs used in Traditional Chinese Medicine by the Connecticut Institute of Herbal Studies.
*Note: Compounded means combined, (in listing of herbal remedies). The symbol * denotes Chinese herbs.

ADRENAL INSUFFICIENCY: Licorice Root has a specific use for this problem along with Fresh Wild Oats, Licorice Root, *Siberian Ginseng, Fo-Ti Extract, and as described in the chapter *Signs of Aging*, Wild Yam. Eating good amounts of sea vegetables or taking kelp and cereal grass supplements will help support the adrenals. Stress relieving herbs that can reduce strain on the adrenals are Hops, Passionflower, Skullcap and *Ginseng. The flower remedy, Calming Essence can also reduce stress.

AGE SPOTS: These are nothing more than accumulated cellular debris, not being able to find an easy way out of the body, they lodge in the skin. Herbal helpers can include Dandelion, *Ginseng, Gotu Kola, Licorice and Sarsaparilla. Bilberry also helps slow the aging process because it is an anti-oxidant, stabilizes connecting tissue and strengthens blood vessels.

ANXIETY: Fear and anxiety can become a real handicap for women in menopause who now become afraid of elevators, airplanes, stuffy rooms and the like. Flower remedies in a combination of Aspen, Mimulus, Blackberry, Cherry Plum, Red Chestnut and Rock Rose along with Garlic give almost immediate relief from panic attacks. Herbal treatments include Compounded Elixir of Passionflower, Compounded Skullcap/St. John's Wort, Compounded Melissa. Probotanixx's *An Shen (includes Zizyphus, Polygonum, Albizzia, Hoelen, Cnidium, Schizandra, Coptis, Anemarrhena, Rehmannia, Licorice). Homeopathic remedies include Gelsemium sempervirens. Bee pollen has had a relaxing effect on some people and may help with anxiety. Also refraining from intake of sugars, caffeine, alcohol or other stimulants will reduce the triggers that cause these attacks.

ARTHRITIS: A home treatment could include the following procedure. In the morning, drink a half a glass of raw potato juice on an empty stomach (or dilute with warm water). Eat organic foods. An hour before lunch eat 2-3 Juniper berries. After lunch eat 2-4 whole mustard seeds. During the day drink the water organic potatoes were boiled in. Cabbage juice as well as black cherry juice, also

109

have been known to reduce the symptoms of arthritis. Taking extra calcium and magnesium and drinking goats milk may improve the condition.

Herbs that can help are Una de Gato, Compounded Red Clover, Nettles, Compounded Yucca/Burdock and Compounded Devil's Claw/Chaparral and instead of eating Juniper berries, take them in a liquid herbal tincture. There are specific herbal agents that influence certain kinds of arthritis and you should consult an herbologist for these.

If you have bearing-down type of pain in the lower back combined with a tired feeling, you may consider a homeopathic tissue salt, Calc. Fluor. (Calcium Fluoride) which helps to preserve the power of elastic tissue to contract. Mag. Phos. (Magnesium Phosphate) is also good for steady sharp neuralgic pains in the back as it is an anti-spasmodic. Garlic, nutritional yeast and kelp can help pain and cayenne pepper can help the joints to be more flexible. For lower back pain use *Wen Yang (Modified Eucommia and Rehmannia formula)

BALDNESS OR THINNING HAIR: Depending on what has caused the condition, these treatments may work. Rinse the scalp with vinegar and Sage tea. Take 40 drops of liquid Red Clover tops daily and 30-60 mg. of zinc. You can also rub aloe vera in the scalp. Another treatment is to drink tea on a daily basis, made from Stinging Nettle, Walnut leaves and Elder leaves. Rub the bald part frequently with the 1/4 pint of onion juice mixed with water, half an ounce of Pearlash, one-eighth of a pint of rum and twenty drops of oil of Rosemary until it looks red. Biochemic cell salt treatment can include Kali. Sulph. (Potassium Sulphate) for falling-out hair and bald spots as well as Nat. Mur. (Sodium Chloride). Bee pollen has worked for some people who not only had their hair grow back, but it turned gray back to color. To help restore hair color use *Shou Wu Chih (Radix Polygoni Multifori).

GOUT: Black cherry juice can help gouty arthritis. You can also apply a poultice of chopped fresh onions daily. Yucca and Devil's Claw Leaves, Chaparral, Fresh Pipsissewa Herb, Fresh Juniper Berry, Fresh Stinging Nettle Leaf, Burdock and Ginkgo are also helpful. You can also chew grains of mustard seeds and drink a strong infusion of Elder Buds in the morning and evening.

HIGH BLOOD PRESSURE: When older persons suffer from high blood pressure, they should reduce their intake of cheese, peas, beans, eggs, highly seasoned foods and meat and add asparagus, buckwheat and brown rice, since they tend to reduce blood pressure. Garlic is an excellent remedy for this ailment. You can also mix one half a teaspoon of cream of tartar, two tablespoons sulphur and two tablespoons of Epsom salts in one quart of water and take two tablespoons of this daily.

HOT FLASHES: Drink tea containing Sage, Lady's mantle and Horsetail. Take a combination of cod liver oil, vitamin E with C, evening Primrose Oil supplements and gamma oryzanol (within rice bran oil). Herbs that have been effective in some women include, Dong Quai, *Ginseng, Black Cohosh, Blue Cohosh, Hawthorn, Unicorn and False Unicorn Root, Wild Yam Root, Chaste Berry and *Licorice Root, Compounded Sage, Motherwort and Peppermint and Compounded Vitex/Alfalfa. The homeopathic approach suggests taking Lachesis for severe hot flashes and Pulsatilla for milder ones. Examining if foods trigger hot flashes and avoid eating those that cause symptoms.

INSOMNIA: Depending on the cause of the insomnia, you can try soothing music and soaking your feet in a solution of hot water and vinegar. Avoid eating big meals and stimulant types of foods before retiring. You can also make a brew of one teaspoon of plain gelatin in one cup of boiling water and take two teaspoons of this with dinner. Warm milk may be beneficial as it releases natural tryptophan. Herbs that may help are Compounded Elixir of Passionflower, Compounded Skullcap/St. John's Wort, Hope, Vervain, Valerian, Catnip, Peppermint and Golden Seal. Oatseed is soothing and supporting of the nervous system and alleviates depression, insomnia and anxiety. Royal jelly is effective for insomnia. Biochemic remedies include Nat. Phos. (Sodium Phosphate) in alternation with Nat. Sulph. (Sodium Sulphate) when due to digestive disturbances, and Kali. Phos. (Potassium Phosphate), when insomnia stems from nervousness or over-excitement.

MALE SYMPTOMS: Three herbs from the Amazon can act as aphrodisiacs and have been used for impotence: Marapuama, Catuaba and Cajueiro with Marapuama being most effective for erectile dysfunctions. Chewing on ginseng root daily helps along with taking the herbs, Damiana, Fo-Ti, Gotu-Kola, Sarsaparilla, Saw Palmetto, and *Shou Wu Chih formula (Radix Polygoni Multifori). Bee pollen also can improve sperm production and increase sexual libido. Prostate inflammation can be helped by Compounded Saw Palmetto, Fresh Thuja Leaf, Compounded Echinacea, Pau d'Arco, Jatoba, Burdock, Cornsilk, Couch Grass, Uva Ursi, Buchu Leaves, Juniper Berries and Marshmallow. Homeopathic treatments include Mag. Phos. (Magnesium Phosphate) and Nat. Sulph. (Sodium Phosphate).

OSTEOPOROSIS: Herbal treatments include drinking a tea three times a day of Wild Oats, Nettles, Marshmallow Root, Yellow Dock and Horsetail (silica). Osteoporosis must be prevented through proper diet and supplementation as described previously in this book. The addition of bee pollen, royal jelly, calcium and magnesium, Vitamin C, D, K and trace elements, especially Boron will help to guard against this disease. (see chapter, "Signs of Aging")

VARICOSE VEINS: Drink three cups daily of white oak bark tea, and take garlic and vitamin E supplements. To relieve the pain, bathe the legs in vinegar three times daily. Taking the cell salt Calc. Fluor. (Calcium Fluoride) will help to restore the elasticity to the vein and cause contraction.

YOUTH: The youth producing hormone is reduced by 80% at age 75 therefore supplementation seems to be a wise decision. DHEA is rapidly becoming known as the anti-aging miracle of the 21st Century. Produced by the adrenal glands, it is converted to other hormones in the body regulating diabetes, obesity, carcinogenesis, tumor growth, virus and bacterial infection, stress, pregnancy, hypertension, collagen and skin integrity, fatigue, depression, memory and immune responses. A lack of the hormone can cause stress these areas and more. Supplementing your diet with DHEA, manufactured from non-animal cholesterol (vegetable sterol), may have the following benefits: lowers cholesterol, retards arterial plaque, increases fat metabolism, reverses diabetes, prevents fat storage, lowers risk of rheumatoid arthritis, restores memory, guards against osteoporosis and prostate problems, increases sexual libido, lifts depression and taken indiscriminately. Recommended dosages (normally between 5 and 50 mg) should be strictly adhered to unless under the care of a practicioner familiar with DHEA. For more information refer to DHEA: Unlocking the Secrets to the Fountain of Youth, by Beth M. Ley. in the resource directory.

If you have been reading this book diligently and taking the information to heart, you might well be on the road to reversing the aging process by keeping a clean healthy body. In this chapter we will discuss the main tool to be used in creating a youthful you....the mind. How many times have people mentioned to you that "thoughts are things", "be careful what you wish for, because you may get it (good and bad)" and "think positive"? Religions have taught that prayer will spawn miracles. Could it not be collective thought processes actually changing electrons, protons or whatever unseen molecule seems to make things happen? Christian Scientists have built a whole belief system on the power of the mind and they have produced some pretty remarkable results.

A friend, general manager of a major sports team, burned himself horribly when a gas grill flared up in his face. Rather than seek medical help and an arduous recovery which included skin grafting, he left his fate to Christian Scientist friends who kept him in a bedroom, sight unseen for a week. Outside this room they visualized his face as being perfectly recovered, and without pain. They instructed the "patient" to do the same. With very minimal topical applications of some herbal salve and with very strong mind techniques, this man fully recovered without medical help, and today has no scars or trace of his accident.

The medical profession is now acknowledging the power of the mind to heal. The government of the USA just admitted to including psychics on their payroll for espionage purposes. A new medical term 'subtle energies', has recently been invented to describe the effects the mind has on influencing the body, and formed an organization around that theory, the International Society for the Study of Subtle Energies and Energy Medicine (ISSSEEM). Mind control is not new news, its just coming out of the closet. In the following pages, we will mostly discuss how the mind affects the body's ability to make itself sick or well, but if you carry this further, you will see how your thoughts determine whether you become old as you age, or stay young.

Since the baby boomers are all arriving at that magic age where retirement is starting to become a reality, corporate America is responding with media coverage targeting the 'older' person. Nursing homes and retirement communities are advertising on TV and many of them focus on the elderly as being needy, gray, hunched over beings no longer wishing to be a burden on their children. If this is what is implanted in the mind over and over again, what do you think will surface? Expectations beget reality and if you are prone to think that you will shrink and get hunched over by the time you are 70, then you will. On the other hand...like one TV ad shows, you could be in your 70s and still jumping hurdles in a track competition. It's up to you!

This chapter is written in collaboration with Dr. William Lowe Mundy, MD, a personal friend and currently Clinical Professor of Medicine at the University of Missouri School of Medicine in Kansas City. He maintains a private practice specializing in Psychosomatic Disease, Internal Medicine and Psychotherapy and has written a book about his techniques for visual imagery. Through clinical observations, experiments and personal experiences, Dr. Mundy has broadened his approach to healing, to include alternative treatments and recognizing the power of the mind to influence the body's ability to heal or hurt itself. The following text is excerpted from his writings and lectures.

In the last couple of decades we have seen some startling results from research done in a field called psychoneuro-immunology. It is wonderful to think that we can actually voluntarily change our immune system, once thought to be autonomic and not in our control, by utilizing specific kinds of thought patterns.

A group of volunteers can have regular blood counts done at the start of an experiment and the number and kind of white blood cells determined. Shown a slide of white blood cells, they then utilize simple relaxation techniques and for a quiet hour are asked to imagine that they are increasing the number of those cells. At the end of the hour, their blood counts are again determined. There is a highly significant increase in cells. It is even possible to increase not just the total number of white blood cells, but to increase a specific kind.

This imagery is the mind's way of reminding you of the way something looked, sounded, felt, smelled or tasted. We use imagery all the time. If I decide to scratch myself where I itch, I must, of necessity, process the location of the discomfort and then 'image' my finger to go to that place. I have to be in control of that motion from the very inception of the thought of wanting to scratch. In milliseconds, I imagine with my mind's eye how my finger will go to the place I have chosen, and it does!

I used to think of the body as being comprised of different organs, all working together and each having their own special set of cells. This in itself seemed pretty miraculous. What in the world could have been the mediator, who could be the manager, who or what could possibly coordinate all these happenings that make us operate?

Some doctor friends believe these accomplishments are due in some miraculous fashion to a proper mingling of chemicals in the brain that somehow are able to send messages down pathways called motor nerves, those connected serially one to the next with spaces called synapses. Each message would have to go through a series of chemical transactions in order to get to the end organ, and then have the success of the movement transmitted back to the brain by another set of nerves called sensory. I can't imagine how a bunch of chemicals can initiate a thought, a desire to move, and be able to choose just which connecting links are needed to effect the desire.

Think of a really complicated process, like playing the piano. Can you possibly imagine that ten fingers, moving all at once and with amazing deliberate direction, combined with a foot pedal working along with them, motivated in some way through the interpretation of the visual perception processed by the mind off the pages of a musical score, listened to by an auditory mechanism in such a finite way that the hands can place less or more energy to the keys dependent on the congruency of the comfort level of the performer, changing speed, tone and timbre at will, of even remotely believing that such amazing coordination could be under the control of a bunch of chemicals??!!

A group of patients suffering from cancer are instructed to construct in their mind their own cartoon-like picture of their own cancer cells, and again image a picture of what they think their immune cells can do to eradicate the cancer cells. They then practice this little play in their mind for an extended period of time, and sure enough it is found that these patients do far better in ameliorating and sometimes curing their cancers than the non-imagers. Are those results due to a set of chemicals?

What we know as a placebo effect is now accepted as real by the medical profession. What amazing things must have happened between mind and body to explain how someone is given a prescription (placebo) by Great Father Doctor, believing it would be of benefit and sure enough, they got well? To think that we never stopped to investigate how come a placebo worked!

How you think (processing pieces of information) results in how you feel (the emotions you have following your thinking), and ends up causing a change in the body. For instance something goes wrong (you think), and you get so 'up tight' emotion) that your blood pressure rises (physical manifestation). Emotional reactions of all sorts create bodily responses of organs not connected by nerve pathways. Continued stress somehow alerts the adrenals to produce more steroids, the liver to start producing more glycogen, the spleen to get more cells into action; all miraculously working together to preserve our wellness.

Most of us have simply accepted that our body's responses to our emotions are automatic and yet we have all experienced a time when we taught ourselves to defy these emotions and got a different result. We have the power, the capacity, to feel miserable as well as happy. For most of us it is easy to 'image' a person and circumstances to have what is called a sexual fantasy. We can utilize a goal-oriented scheme in our mind to change the function of our body, by imaging the parts we wish to contact and sending those parts a message.

All too often doctors are prone to believe that emotional problems, such as depression, occur as a result of disease. I believe that emotions can also cause a disease. Most people don't realize that they learned a long time ago to have the depression they suffer with today. Whatever you were taught, whatever learnings you incorporated as a child, can be unlearned. If one feels helpless and victimized by fate and their own sense of inadequacy, the immune system would be hard put to be of much help with visual imagery, therefore these feelings and the resultant depression must be resolved before visual imagery can work. Several years ago I met two women who had Lupus Erythematosis and who became aware of the relationship of their depression and their disease. With devoted effort they not only cured their depression, they stopped having the disease.

I have been successful ridding people of their allergies by visual imagery. Somewhere along the line our immune systems decided the good guys (tourists) were bad guys (terrorists) and decided to fight them...thus, a la, allergies. Through simple imagery, we can re-educate the immune system to embrace the tourists and not confuse them with the terrorists, thereby getting rid of our allergic reactions. If you don't believe some allergies are created in the mind, explain why many allergic people sneeze at pictures of flowers, when there is absolutely no pollen around.

Quality of life is important to maintain as we age and we all want health, happiness (and money) in our later years. Goal setting and taking an Anthony Robbins course may get you the money and some happiness, but you have to create your own good health. According to the relevant literature, psychological factors may play an important role in the onset and clinical course of rheumatoid arthritis, a common ailment in older persons. Studies have shown that joint tenderness from arthritis is more prevalent in patients with lower levels of self-esteem.

Unhappy emotions and poor self-image can lead to disease. In one study on patients with multiple sclerosis, 28 of the 32 people interviewed revealed that their transition into MS coincided with a psychologically stressful situation, one which mobilized feelings of helplessness. Since multiple sclerosis is commonly thought to be related at least in part to alterations in the immune system, it is possible to speculate that immune mechanisms which are already compromised, can undergo further destabilization under some circumstances, in the face of severe or chronic emotional upset. "Does this mean we play a part in creating disease?"

I am sure there are many patients, along with their doctors, who are unwilling to believe that they can be a part of their own cure. They may be unwilling to deal with their own emotional states and would be loath to undertake a therapeutic approach, in which they would have to stop viewing themselves as victims and would be asked to take an aggressive role in their healing. Visual imagery is a completely normal and necessary process used by every person every day. All we are doing with a more therapeutic process is to design a goal-oriented method of contacting parts of the body that we here-to-fore have considered unavailable. Visual imagery makes it possible for us to take part in our own health and well-being. It is easy to do and completely harmless. The power of the mind can be curative. Using new thoughts, re-perceptions, imaging in innovative ways, upon re-framing, healing can be done within the mind without verbalization or conversation with a therapist.

As people age, they seem to accept that their bodies are bound to deteriorate and that they are at risk for debilitating illness. By practicing imagery, as described in the book, *Curing Allergy with Visual Imagery*, you can change that thought and create for yourself a different consequence. In using imagery to cure allergies, I ask my patients to think of themselves as Disney cartoonists. Getting away from realism is easier for most people to do. It relieves them of the need to be perfect and makes the imaging a fun kind of thing. We know that the information is understood by the cells no matter how incongruous someone's idea of what magnified elements might look like. It is the ideas behind the imagery plot that we want to get across and accuracy of method doesn't seem to be significant. Perhaps the immune system likes a happier, yet effective way of going about the job.

If you are not willing to buy into this concept of the way our mind, body and spirit work together and of the mind being present in all of our parts, then explain in your own way how the outcome of imagery when used to change cellular function, definitely works. I can find no other way to explain such marvelous happenings. And think of it this way, to quote Richard Bach, "Not knowing doesn't keep the truth from being true". Remember, "you are what you think". We highly recommend reading *"Curing Allergy With Visual Imagery"* by Wm. Lowe Mundy. Available through (800)-272-2000.

Another technique for rejuvenating the body, mind and spirit comes from Kaya Kalpa, one of the ancient sciences of India. It sets forth a precise method using very sophisticated understanding of the characteristics of certain herbal combinations. These herbs stimulate the body and mind at very subtle levels opening up blockages in the nervous system's centers of energy (chakras). This allows the body to rebuild its seven layers described in Ayur Veda, India's science of life. Restoring energy flow throughout the body, provides the mind with the nutrients it needs to complete the process of regeneration.

FITNESS FOR YOUTH..

Beginning a fitness program can be as easy as taking a walk every day. Walking is a natural movement for the body and helps to strengthen bone and muscle as it exercises the heart and lungs. As we age, even as early as 35, we begin to lose muscle mass and about 1% of bone mass per year. For post menopausal women, the percentage may as much as quadruple. Beginning an exercise program that includes weight bearing exercises such as walking, cycling and running, can not only increase your muscle and bone mass, but decrease your body fat as well. Walking at a pace that elevates your heart rate is considered an aerobic activity. This exercises the heart and lungs and this puts you at a lower risk level for diabetes, heart disease, hypertension, and osteoporosis.

It's always a good idea to check with your physician before beginning any exercise program.

To get on your way to feeling wonderfully fit and healthy, start your walking program today! You'll need a good pair of walking shoes and comfortable clothes. Layering is always a good idea. A good way to get in tune with your body is by feeling how hard you are working. Familiarize yourself with your perceived exertion level. Zero is standing still and ten is when you are almost out of breath. You should strive for a level of 6 to 8 which means you should be able to carry on a conversation without becoming breathless. If this is happening to you, slow your pace down a bit. Strive for 60-70%.

AGE	MAX. HEART RATE	60%	70%
30	195	115	133
40	180	110	126
50	170	105	119
60	160	95	112
70	150	85	105
80	140	75	98

To begin you program you should walk at a comfortable pace for about five minutes, stop and stretch your calves, hamstrings, and quadriceps, holding each stretch for about twenty seconds. The reason for walking before you stretch is to warm up the muscles. Stretching cold muscles can lead to injury so be sure to walk first, then stretch.

Quad stretch

Calf stretch

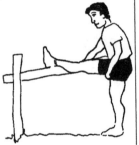
Hamstring stretch

Select a program that is right for you from the following: Beginner level: walk for 15-20 minutes, 3 times/week Intermediate: walk for 25-45 minutes, 4-5 times/week Advanced: walk for 45-60 minutes, 5-7 times/week. If you're a beginner, stay with the first program until you find it too easy, and increase your time gradually. Also, remember to drink plenty of water. Staying hydrated when you exercise is very important, especially in hot weather!

A fun way to increase your endurance and put variety in you work out is to use "fartlek", a Swedish word meaning speedplay. During your walk, look for mailboxes, telephone poles, driveways, etc., and increase your speed from one to the next. For example, after you've walked for about ten minutes, walk fast from one driveway to the next, then resume your normal pace. Do this up to ten times during your walk. Once this becomes easy, try increasing your pace for two driveways then three, etc. It's fun and it helps you to stay motivated.

If you want to try something more challenging and your physician tells you it's OK to run, try walking for two minutes, then jog or run for one. (of course, this is after you've warmed up and stretched). Another challenge is to switch your walking time to one minute and run for two, or walk two and run two. There are lots of ways to keep from getting bored. The main objective is to have fun and enjoy what you're doing.

If possible, try to vary your course or walk up hills to challenge your body. Variety wards off boredom, so try to change the scenery or walk with a friend to keep things interesting. If you find yourself short on time, a ten minute walk can do wonders for you mentally and any time spent exercising is better than none at all. When you've completed your walk, be sure to stretch the same muscles you did after your warm up. This will prevent soreness and help to keep you injury free.

An important component of exercise for those over fifty is strength training. For each decade of life, adults lose approximately six pounds of muscle. Muscle strength decreases by about twenty percent by age sixty-five along with a decrease in flexibility. Regular strength training not only prevents some of this loss, but increases bone and muscle mass and flexibility. Studies have shown that a regular strength training program can add about three pounds of muscle mass in approximately two months. Researchers in Gainsville, Florida had men and women, ranging in age from sixty to eighty-two exercise for six months, using special back strengthening machines. The results showed that their spinal bone density increased by fourteen percent. This is especially significant for women because they lose ten to fifteen percent of the minerals needed to sustain bone in their spines during the ten years following menopause.

Strength training for women and men over fifty is critical to staying active in later years. Bones need to be subjected to stress in order to increase density and generate bone growth. Lifting weights provides the stress needed to do this while muscles, tendons, and ligaments become stronger. Your sense of balance is improved along with reaction time, both of which help prevent falls. Fractured hips and spines are all too common occurrences in those over 65, and a basic strength training program can help prevent this. Beginning now can help you look and feel great, plus help keep you healthy and strong for years to come!

Many of us have a problem with weight gain as we get older, and although aerobic exercise is one way to lose weight, research has shown that a combination of aerobics and strength training is the best way to reduce body fat. Although you may expend more calories during aerobic activities, the rate at which you burn calories (metabolic rate) remains elevated for a longer period of time following strength training. Your body expends thirty to fifty calories just maintaining the muscle you are building!

To begin a strength training program, you'll want to plan on working out two to three times per week. It's important to wait at least twenty four hours before working the same muscles again. Muscles need adequate time to recover and rebuild. The following program is designed to work major muscle groups in approximately twenty to thirty minutes, however, if you want to increase your strength, you can simply do two to three sets instead of one. The American

College of Sports Medicine recommends eight to ten exercises for major muscle groups, eight to twelve repetitions with a minimum of one set, and exercising a minimum of two times per week.
* Again, always check with your physician before starting an exercise program.

Be sure to warm up your muscles first with some sort of rhythmic limbering by walking, marching in place, walking on a treadmill, using a stationary bike, dancing to music...whatever you like to do for five to ten minutes. Follow this with static stretches for the major muscle groups. Hold each stretch for at least twenty seconds, and be careful not to bounce.! Begin with large muscle groups and progress to smaller muscles for a safe, well- rounded program.

Additional Stretches:

After you have warmed up, begin each exercise slowly, taking one to two seconds for each movement, exhaling with exertion.

1. Stand with your knees unlocked, feet should be a shoulder width apart and toes pointed out. Hold a resistance band (like a giant flat rubber band), in your hands and lift both hands overhead, pulling out, creating resistance against the bands. Keeping abdominals contracted, pull arms down and back while you do a slight knee bend. Return to beginning position. Do 8-12 repetitions. This works the back (latissimus dorsi) and lower body.

2. With your hands on your hips, or at your sides, holding 1-3 lb. weights, lunge forward with the right leg. Modify this exercise by making a small lunge (or lunge backward if you have a problem with your knees). Do not let your knees go in front of your toes. Do 8-12 with each leg. This exercise works the front of the thighs (quadriceps), back of leg (hamstrings) and buttocks (gluteals).

3. Lie on your side, with legs extended, and your head resting on your forearm, the other hand on floor in front of your chest. You may use 1-3 lb. ankle weights. Flex foot and lift your leg to about hip level, being careful not to roll back. Lower the leg back to floor. Do 8-10 repetitions then repeat with the other leg. This works the outer thigh muscles (abductors).

4. Stay on your side and drop the top leg in front of you on the floor. Lift the back leg up to work the inner thigh muscles. return it to the floor. Do this 8-10 times and repeat with the other leg, being careful not to roll back. The most effective way to do this exercise is slowly, pausing for a moment at the top. Works the hip adductors.

5. On "all fours", with ankle weights, resistance bands or nothing at all, with abdominals contracted, keeping your back flat, rest on your forearms, keeping your knees under your hips, lift and straighten one leg, then slowly bend the knee so that your heel curls toward the buttocks. Straighten the leg. Do 8-12 before repeating with other leg. Be careful not to arch your back. This works the back of the leg (hamstrings).

6A. Lay on your back with your knees bent, and your hands across your chest or behind the head with elbows out. Think of having an orange under your chin to prevent you from pushing your chin onto your chest as you raise. Tighten abdominals and lift your shoulders off floor while bringing a knee toward your chest. Do 10 - 30 reps, alternating legs. Exhale as you lift up. This works the upper and lower muscles of the abdominals.

6B. To work the obliques (waist muscles) , stay on your back with your knees bent and cross the right ankle over the left knee. With your hands behind your head, keep the right elbow on floor and lift diagonally while exhaling, bringing the left shoulder (not elbow) toward the knee. Return to the floor. Do 8-15 reps on each side.

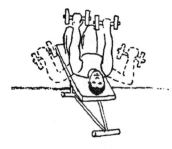

7. Stay on your back with your knees bent and abdominals contracted. Hold resistance bands or 1-3 lb. weights in both hands and raise your arms towards the ceiling with your hands almost touching. Move your arms out and down until your elbows touch the floor, exhaling as you go. Slowly bring the arms back up to your beginning position. Do 8-12 reps. This works the chest (pectoralis muscles).

8. In a face down position, contract the lower back muscles and lift the chest off the floor, using the arms slightly to assist you. Hold for a moment, and then return to starting position. Be careful not to overextend the lower back, or to throw the head back while lifting. Do 8 reps. This works the low back.

9. Stand up, with your feet a hip width apart, abdominals contracted, and your arms at your sides, palms up. Hold 1-3 lb. weight in each hand, if desired. Keeping elbows tight against sides, curl your hands up to your shoulders, exhaling as you lift, then slowly lower to starting position. Don't swing weights. Do 8-12 reps. This works the biceps.

10. Remaining in the same position, and holding 1-3 lb. weights at your sides, palms in, lift your arms our to your sides just to shoulder level, elbows slightly bent, exhaling as you lift. Slowly lower back down to sides. Do 8-12 reps. This works the shoulders (deltoids).

11. To do triceps dips, sit on an armless chair, with your hands holding the front of the seat, with fingers pointing down. Move forward until your hips come off the chair, and lower buttocks to the floor. Press up with your arms for full extension, arms straight, but not locked. Keep feet firmly on the floor with knees bent. Repeat 8 -12 times. This works the back of arms (triceps).

To complete your strength training program, it's important to finish by stretching the muscles you've just worked. This will prevent soreness, help to resume normal resting length of the muscle and increase flexibility. You should enjoy your time spent stretching. Repeat the stretches given at the beginning of this chapter, holding each for at least twenty to thirty seconds.

Relaxation is a wonderful bonus to add to your workout when you have time. You'll find it relieves tension and stress and gives you renewed energy. Find a quiet spot or play some relaxing music. Think of your mind as a blackboard and erase all writing on the board to clear you mind. Imagine yourself in a place that you love, perhaps the beach, hearing the waves gently rolling to shore, feeling the warmth of the sun on your body. Take deep, diaphragmatic breaths (belly breathing), and exhale very slowly. Try to think of the peaceful sensation you are feeling as a color, bathing you slowly from head to toe. Beginning at your feet, relax muscle by muscle, pausing at each one to enjoy the feeling. Continue to breathe deeply and slowly. When you feel completely relaxed, think of something that makes you happy, that makes you smile. Bring it to the front of your mind and keep it there until the next time you do this exercise. Staying active can help us live our lives to their fullest.

RESOURCE DIRECTORY..

DETOXIFICATION:

ALL NATURAL TOXIN REMOVAL. ARISE & SHINE'S Clean-Me-Out Program™, as developed by Dr. Richard Anderson, N.D., N.M.D., is the most effective, all-natural way of removing toxins and unwanted waste materials from the body today. These toxins build up in layers in the colon and intestines, and prevent the body from properly absorbing vitamins and health supplements. Common reported benefits from The Clean-Me-Out detoxification program are: improved health, more energy, greater clarity of mind, improved stamina, better skin tone and improved physiological functions. Free catalogue/information packet available. ARISE & SHINE HERBAL PRODUCTS, 3225 N. Los Altos, Tucson, AZ 85705 (800)-688-2444

ACIDOPHILUS FOR A HEALTHY COLON: Staying healthy is not easy in this day and age. Busy lifestyles, prescription drugs and hormonal changes often lead to digestive troubles, fatigue and yeast infections. PB 8 Pro-Biotic Acidophilus helps keep your system in tip-top condition by maintaining optimum levels of good bacteria. PB 8 contains eight strains of friendly bacteria per capsule, 14 billion count at the time of manufacture and requires no refrigeration. Nutrition Now's Natural Menopause is another product that helps with the symptoms of menopause such as hot flashes, fatigue, stress, anxiety and mood swings. while replenishing the body with vitamins and herbs. NUTRITION NOW, INC., 501 SE Columbia Shores Blvd., Bldg. 350, Vancouver, WA 98661 (800)-929-0418

IMMUNE SYSTEM SUPPORT:

AGED GARLIC EXTRACT, GREENS AND ACIDOPHILUS: Choosing an appropriate garlic supplement can be a confusing process. Actually, there are 4 choices: (1) heat distilled garlic oil in softgels, (2)heat dehydrated garlic seasoning powder in capsules/tablets, (3) garlic oil macerates and (4) KYOLIC odorless Aged Garlic Extract™. All garlic supplements probably have some nutritional value, but oils and powders do not contain significant amounts of water soluble compounds which are essential to retain all of the benefits of garlic. Garlic oils and powders contain smelly oil soluble sulphur compounds which cause pungent garlic odor as well as harsh oxidizing side effects.. Since the development of Kyolic® almost four decades ago, more research has been done on this Aged Garlic Extract, than on all other garlic supplements combined. Kyolic® is also covered by more than a dozen patents and patents pending worldwide. See the chapter "Garlic" for the benefits of Aged Garlic Extract (AGE). The makers of Kyolic® also provide a comprehensive powdered "green" drink which includes young barley and wheat grasses grown in the pristine Nasu Highlands in Japan, cooked brown rice, chlorella from natural mineral springs, and kelp from the Northern Pacific. This combination provides you with a daily balanced amount of greens. Also necessary for the body, is the addition of L.acidophilus, B.bifidum and B.longum strains of live "friendly" bacteria found in Kyo-Dophilus® used in 30,000 hospitals and clinics. This product is heat stable (needs no refrigeration) and therefore is excellent for traveling. It is human grade therefore is bioavailable in the digestive tract. This makes it an safe product for all ages.. Another product, Acidophilase™ combines the "friendly" bacteria with enzymes, amylase, lipase and protease. These products are all yeast, sodium and dairy free and are available at your local stores or through WAKUNAGA OF AMERICA, 23501 Madero, Mission Viejo, CA 92691 (800)-825-7888

NUTRITIONAL YEAST SUPPLEMENTS: Bio-Strath, a Swiss quality product from Bioforce is a natural food supplement for all people. It is made from a unique combination of plasmolyzed nutritional yeast and wild herbs, free from any synthetic additives and preservatives. These yeast cells have essential substances in a balanced composition including proteins, fats, carbohydrates, minerals, enzymes and amino-acids and these supplements come in either a liquid or tablet form. BioForce also makes a full line of herbal and homeopathic products. BIOFORCE OF AMERICA, LTD., Smith Rd., Kinderhook, NY 12106 (800)-445-8802

LIQUID CRYSTALLOID MINERALS: Trace-Lyte™ is a true crystalloid (smallest form in nature) electrolyte formula that helps maintain the body's primary bio-oxidation process. It raises the

Osmotic Pressure of the cell walls, strengthening them! It changes back the pH of the cell to its healthy state. This process is generally referred to as homeostasis (electrolyte balance). High absorption is achieved due to its crystalloid structure. Some doctors have even said it acts like 'chelation' in a bottle! Unlike most earth-type liquid minerals, there is no heavy metal contaminates whatsoever. NATURE'S PATH, INC. PO Box 7862, Venice FL 34287-7862 (800)-326-5772, (941)-426-3375 fax (941)-426-6871

WHOLE FOOD CONCENTRATES IN SUPPLEMENT FORM:
MegaFood™ uses Mother Nature to actually grow highly potent Whole Food Vitamin and Mineral Concentrates. Researchers have discovered that vitamins and minerals should be an integral part of an unrefined complex in order to achieve optimum absorption and subsequent health benefits. GrowForm™ nutrients comes very close to this natural structure. They are whole-food concentrates produced by a growing process which results in a nutrient-dense complex similar to food, making them among the most bioavailable of all supplements. One-Daily™ is a full spectrum, multivitamin/ mineral supplement designed for those who like the convenience of taking one tablet a day. IMMUCAN™ has been carefully researched and designed to give your immune system a nutritional, strengthening boost by including Vitamin C, Beta Carotene, Super Oxide Dismutase (S.O.D.), Glutathione Peroxidase, Co-Enzyme Q-10, Acidophilus and 17 herbs. BIO SAN LABORATORIES, INC., 8 Bowers Road., Derry NH 03038 (800)-258-5014

ALL NATURAL BROAD-SPECTRUM MICRONUTRIENTS:
The stresses of increasing micronutrient deficiencies in the diet can accelerate aging and depress the immune system. Ocean plants (seaweeds and kelp) naturally concentrate nature's richest source of chelated minor trace minerals and other micronutrients. Micronutrient supplementation has been shown to benefit allergies, immune response, hair growth, energy levels, and other symptoms of aging. MICRO-MAX is produced by the company that has innovated unique processing and blending techniques to preserve maximum micronutrient activity. SOURCE, INC., 101 Fowler Rd., N. Branford, CT 06471 (800)-232-2365

ELECTROLYTE CALCIUM SUPPLEMENTS WITH BORON:
Many health authorities have recently stated that osteoporosis is reaching epidemic proportions in our country! This appears to be happening to men as well as women. Recently, research has shown that by supplementing our diets with good quality 1 to 1 ratio of calcium and magnesium, we may not only stop the thinning of our bones, but in fact, rebuild them! Cal-Lyte™ with electrolytes and boron can give you this assurance and its super absorption formula can reduce muscle soreness, all forms of cramping and low back pain. . NATURE'S PATH, INC., PO Box 7862, Venice, FL 34287-7862 (800)-326-5772

FLAX SEED IN EASY TO USE FORM: Flax seed contains an abundant balance of Omega-3 and Omega-6 essential fatty acids, along with soluble and insoluble fiber and lignins. Therefore, it provides you with the best natural health package to balance, normalize and rejuvenate your body. Omega Life's "Fortified Flax" provides you with an easy to use flax meal with vitamins and minerals to help your body metabolize its wealth of benefits. It is also stabilized by a patented process to maintain freshness. "Fortified Flax" can be sprinkled on cereal, mixed with foods, bakery items, etc. and even added to your pet's food. You can also add to juice, their Power Pack Energy Drink Mix, which includes Fortified Flax, oat bran, barley, beta-carotene and lecithin or munch on Omega Bars to get your source of Omega-3's. OMEGA-LIFE, INC., PO Box 208, Brookfield, WI 53008-0208 (800) EAT-FLAX (328-3529).

pH TESTING PAPERS: pH Hydrion Papers test the acid/alkaline condition of your urine. With readings of 5.5 to 8.0, these strips can indicate balance in the body and determine which food to eat to rebalance your system. LONG LIFE CATALOG CO., 132 W. Pocono Tr., Nokomis, FL. 34275 (888)-NATURE-1

SUPPLEMENT COMBINATIONS FOR WOMEN AND MEN:
JUST FOR WOMEN has what every woman needs to maintain a healthy, energetic and active lifestyle. This special formulation not only contains a potent amount of needed vitamins and minerals, but also combines nutrients promoting cellular production of ATP, the "energy molecule", resulting in increased energy. ULTRA MALE provides specific nutrients needed by men combining vitamins and

minerals in a complex that delivers the energy, daily maintenance and emotional uplift needed. It contains major antioxidants, full spectrum minerals, herbal extracts and super energy nutritional concentrates. MEMOR ALL provides a comprehensive range of neurotransmitter precursors plus potent traditional herbs. PURE SOURCE, Miami Beach, FL (800)-324-6273 ·

ANTIOXIDANT & PROTEALYTIC DIGESTIVE ENZYMES. "Cell Guard" is an antioxidant enzyme product made entirely of specially developed organically grown IsoSproutPlex™. Each caplet contains concentrated plant enzymes and Isoflavanoids which neutralize free radicals. "Bio-Gestin" is a protealytic digestive product made entirely from papaya pacifica containing the two protealytic enzymes, papain and chymopapain. The unique property of green papaya helps support the proper operation of the human digestive system. Another excellent antioxidant product by this company, is "Pacific Sea Plasma". It is a renown spirulina grown in Hawaii, known as phyto-plankton which is extremely high in beta carotene, GLA and Vitamin B-12. AGRIGENIC FOODS CORP., 1503 Landing Ave., Seal Beach, CA 90740 (800)-788-1084

WHEAT OR BARLEY GRASS SUPPLEMENTS: Pines Wheat and Barley Grass are naturally concentrated whole food supplements containing generous amounts of vitamins, minerals, anti-oxidants, protein and chlorophyll. The nutritional analysis of Pines Wheat or Barley Grass is much like that of a dark green leafy vegetable, but much more concentrated. Seven tablets or one teaspoon of powder, equals the nutrition found in a large serving of vegetables, such as a large spinach salad. Pines powders are 100% pure and the tablets are 98% pure and free of fillers or other ingredients that dilute the natural potency of the product. Pines has also recently produced "Mighty Greens" which contains a blend of wheat, barley, rye and oat grass along with spirulina, alfalfa and other herbs. PINES INTERNATIONAL, INC., PO Box 1107, Lawrence, KS 66044 (800)-697-4637

BIOAVAILABLE PLANT ENZYMES:. TYME ZYME™ is a unique, highly concentrated enzyme formula for human consumption. TYME ZYME™ contains lipase, amylase, protease, cellulase and lactase enzymes in capsule form. PROZYME™ contains the protease, amylase, lipase and cellulase enzymes in powder form. Scientifically proven to increase the bioavailability and absorption of the vitamins, minerals, fatty acids and other vital nutrients in foods adding enzymes to your diet helps to slow the aging process. PROZYME is great to add to your cat or dog's diet too. PROZYME™ PRODUCTS, LTD. 6600 N. Lincoln Ave., Suite 312, Lincolnwood, IL 60645, (800)-522-5537

ESSENTIAL FATTY ACIDS: Fats, in particular Essential Fatty Acids (EFAs) are a necessary component of a healthy diet. Flax Oil, Evening Primrose Oil and Borage Oil are excellent plant sources of EFAs which are so important for optimal health and well-being. These EFA-rich food oils are available from Health From The Sun, the leader in EFA nutrition. Their flax, evening primrose and borage oils are extracted without the use of any chemical solvents such as hexane. Instead, the cold Expeller-press method is used for oil extraction. Health From The Sun oils are processed according to pharmaceutical standards and are pure enough to exceed the World Health Organization's standards for edible oils. HEALTH FROM THE SUN, PO Box 840, Sunapee, NH 03782 (800)-447-2249

LIQUID CHLOROPHYLL: DeSouza's Liquid Chlorophyll is a versatile product that can be taken as a dietary supplement or used as a mouthwash and breath freshener. It contains no preservatives or flavorings and come in capsules or tablets. Their chlorophyll-based Oral Rinse and Spray is an excellent alcohol free cleansing agent, astringent and breath freshener that is soothing, yet refreshing. Only the purest of water is used, with Ascorbic Acid added as a preservative. Also available is DeSouza's Solar Sea Salt, cured by nature in salt beds and dried by the sun and wind is totally natural, unheated and untreated. DeSOUZA INTERNATIONAL, INC., PO Box 395, Beaumont, CA 92223 (800)-373-5171

PHYTO-HORMONE EXTRACTIONS: A complete line of plant based hormonal supplements for anti-aging therapy. The VITA-DHEA™ formula combines a proprietary blend of specific Dioscorea wild yams from around the world together with a technologically advanced extraction and delivery system. This assures maximum

138

absorption of its active and beneficial phyto-nutrients. VITA-DHEA™ is all natural and virtually free of side effects. All Nutraceutic's products allow the consumer a choice other than synthetic or semi synthetic hormones for anti-aging therapy. NUTRACEUTICS CORP. 600 Fairway Dr. #105, Deerfield Beach, FL 33441 (800)-391-0114

NATURAL AMINO ACIDS: DLPA in/out™ is a natural essential amino acid that helps the body unlock its own healing powers. It an all natural product that reduces the effects of PMS, the swelling and inflammation of arthritis and chronic pains, and depression. CHELOGUARD™ provides a proven combination of oxygen, minerals and vitamins for oral chelation and removing debris from artery walls. It also helps to provide for improved exchange between the arteries and the body's cells, thus allowing better transfer of nutrients and electrolytes. It is used as an adjunct to IV chelation and by-pass surgery. EN GARDE HEALTH PRODUCTS, 7702 Bldg. #10, Balboa Blvd., Van Nuys, CA 91406 (800)- 955-4MED

OXYGEN ENHANCERS: OXY-MOXY™ is an aerobic oxygen enhancer, taken sublingual (under the tongue) and provides more oxygen into the bloodstream from every breath in any environment. It is ideal for people with impaired respiration capabilities and in cases of increased oxygen demand. Clinically proven, it is used by athletes world wide. OXY-HERBS™, is a line of naturally formulated herbs for sublingual use together with OXY-MOXY™ to improve metabolism as each herb is taken,. EN GARDE HEALTH PRODUCTS, 7702 Bldg. #10, Balboa Blvd., Van Nuys, CA 91406 (800)-955-4MED Fax (818)-786-4699. Free catalog, send #10 S.A.S.E. envelope.

100% VEGETARIAN ENZYMES: Nutri-Essence™ Broad Spectrum Enzymes™ help maximize food nutrient value by replacing the enzymes destroyed when food is cooked or processed. These enzymes are 100% vegetarian and are available in VEGICAPS® or great-tasting raspberry chewable tablets.. NUTRI-ESSENCE™ DIV. OF ENZYMES, INC., 100 NW Business Park Lane, Riverside, MO 64150 (800)-647-6377 FAX (800)-844-1957 E-mail NutriEssence@enzymeinc.com

GREEN FOODS: Natural juices can provide you with many essential nutrients in the best form possible, as nature intended. Juice extracts with barley grass, carrots and wheat germ are now available in powdered form.. Discover how GREEN MAGMA, BETA CARROT, and GREEN ESSENCE provides you with live enzymes, beta-carotene, antioxidants, amino acids, detoxifying chlorophyll, essential minerals and more. GREEN FOODS CORP. 318 N Graves Ave. Oxnard, CA 93030 (800)-222-3374 x434

ANTIOXIDANT FORMULA. Vitamins C, E and Beta Carotene is available in a tasty powder form and is 100% vegetarian. A healthy diet supplemented with antioxidants protects against oxidative damage to the body's cells and tissues. Medical science has established that antioxidants reinforce the body's defense against heart disease, lung ailments, arthritis and even cancer. 30-90 day supply available in 66 gm bottle. NICKERSON INTERNATIONAL, LTD. 12 Schubert St. Dept. B, Staten Is., NY 10305 (800)-642-5377

99% PURE ASSAYED DHEA: Known as the hormone that turns back the clock, DHEA helps restore energy, vitality, libido and healthy feeling that age can rob. Fountain of Youth Formula is not derived from wild yams as are some DHEA products. DHEA is a 100% purified cholesterol metabolite recognized in the world's foremost medical journals. Available in 25 and 50 mg. capsules. BODY AMMO NUTRACEUTICALS, 28400 Fox Hollow Dr., Hayward, CA 94542 (800)-346-2303

FLOWERS, HERBS AND BEES:

FLOWER REMEDIES: Calming Essence® is a five flower combination formula used for acute stress, minor tension headaches, cuts, bruises abrasions, etc., and is available in liquid form. EnLighten™ systems are used for emotional relief including weight management, children with learning difficulties, and teen behavior modification. Homeopathy Works™ combines homeopathic formulas for 14 common physical ailments including menopause, arthritis, cough, congested head cold, indigestion, sciatica, lumbago, insomnia, etc. MIGHTY OAK NATURAL PRODUCTS, 10 Bayside Ave., Port Washington, NY 11050 (516)-767-3104

GOOD HEALTH THANKS TO BEES: Pollen is the very source of plant life. It's where nature begins. Nothing is more natural than bee pollen, sometimes called the world's only perfect food. Royal Jelly is rich in amino acids, B-complex vitamins, and is one of the best natural sources of pantothenic acid (Vitamin B-5). Propolis is high in flavonoids and a great variety of phytochemicals. Propolis is gaining worldwide attention for its unique properties. These powerful bee products are very chemically complex and defy complete analysis by science. The High Desert Dynamic Trio® is composed of 520 mg. of Pollenergy, one gram of 24-hour Royal Jelly and 500 mg of Bee Propolis and is available in tablets and vegicaps®.C C POLLEN CO., 3627 E. Indian School Rd., Suite 209, Phoenix, AZ 85018-5126 (800)-875-0096

BRAIN "FOOD": Source Naturals® offers plant-derived Phosphatidyl Serine (PS) in 100 mg. sofgels, and in a brain nutrient complex, Higher Mind™. Source Naturals has a full line of 14 brain nutrition products, including DMAE, Acetyl L-Carnitine, L-Pyroglutamic Acid, Mental Edge®, Mega Mind™ and Ginkgo-24™, a 50-1 standardized concentration of Ginkgo Biloba yielding 24% Ginkgo Flavone Glycosides, in tablet form. Source Naturals' exceptional products are constantly updated and expanded in light of the most recent scientific advances. THRESHOLD ENTERPRISES, 23 Janis Way, Scotts Valley, CA 95066 (800)-815-2333.

SKIN CARE

HERBAL/MINERAL SKIN SPRAY: Skin-Lyte™ is a perfect blend of the best nature has to offer. It encourages rapid absorption of vital mineral nutrients to aid in skin rejuvenation, and is combined with a blend of ancient herbal extracts to help in healing. Skin-Lyte™ is a fusion of crystalloid electrolyte minerals ionically bound with herbal extracts in a base of pure water. Water carries away nutrient, contributes to normal tissue structure, lubricates and flushes away toxins. With consistent use, Skin-Lyte's™ herbs and crystalloid minerals balance pH and provide intense, deep nourishment to the skin aiding healing and rejuvenation. NATURE'S PATH, INC. PO Box 7862, Venice, FL 34287-7862 (800)-326-5772

ALL NATURAL SKIN CARE: Annemarie Börlind produces a complete line of personal care products including facial care, body care, hair care, sun protection, and makeup. The products are botanically based: active ingredients are herbal. The most widely used products are AHA Complex (fruit acids in liposomes), LL Series for mature skin with the unique LL Bio-Complex, System Absolute with liposomes, nanoparticles and superphycodismutase (SPD) which are the latest scientific developments in counteracting free radical damage. They are cruelty-free, biodegradable and have environmentally sound packaging. All products are tested in independent university dermatological clinics on human volunteers to insure safety and efficacy. ANNEMARIE BORLIND OF GERMANY, PO Box 130, New London, NH 03257, (800)-447-7024 Fax (603)-526-2076.

FIVE DROPS TO SKIN HEALTH: These days, it's hard to avoid the harsh elements that can damage skin. Now skin can be defended with Microsomes™ moisturizing drops, beneficial to all skin types. The ingredients include concentrated APT®, Retinol Palmitate, Beta Glucan, Hyaluronic Acid and Pentavitin combined with Glyco/Sphingolipids (a millet seed extract which helps maintain skins' barrier function and prevents moisture loss and increases cell renewal and skin firmness). Also available is Super Skin Zyme Mask, a potent and 100% natural treatment formulated from concentrated green papaya, bromelin, sunflower oil, honey, aloe and vitamin E. It replenishes vital moisture while triggering the skin's renewal mechanism, one which will dissolve dry, dead cells and allow for the rapid development of healthy new ones. LOUISE BIANCO SKIN CARE, INC. 13655 Chandler Blvd., Sherman Oaks, CA 01404 (800)-782-3067

HOMEOPATHIC SKIN CARE REGIMEN: Rejuvennis is the first homeopathic skin care regimen. It is a complete line of all-natural products that beautifully improves the appearance of aging skin while preventing additional damage. Fine lines and wrinkles, adult acne, moisture retention, elasticity and skin tone are dramatically improved as Rejuvennis fights the effects of environmental assaults and aging.

Scientific breakthroughs, using homeopathics, cold processing, and an exclusive Bio-Pathic™ oxygenating system, work in synergy to revitalize and beautify your skin. The all natural homeopathic ingredients include anti-oxidants, enzymes, vitamins, minerals, proteins and more. The results are healthier younger-looking skin without the harsh side effects of chemical based applications, making it great for sensitive skin. It is packaged in distinctive, elegant French crystal pyramid bottles. DREAMOUS, CORP., 505 S.Beverly Dr., Suite 655, Beverly Hills, CA 90212 (800)-251-7543

FOR SUN DAMAGED SKIN AND PRE-MATURE AGING: The beauty of the rose can be yours with Rosa Mosqueta® Rose Hip Seed Oil. Grown high in the Andes Mountains and naturally extracted, Rosa Mosqueta Rose Hip Seed Oil® has been clinically proven to heal the skin and help reduce signs of sun damage and premature aging. It is especially recommended for dry skin. For acne-prone skin, try Green Tea & Green Clay Rejuvenating Facial Mask. Natural fruit acids from bilberry combined with purifying green clay and soothing green tea, make this mask an essential part of your skin care routine. AUBREY ORGANICS, 4419 N. Manhattan Ave., Tampa, FL 33614 (800)-AUBREY H (800-282-7394)

BODY CARE PRODUCTS: Since your skin is the body's largest organ, what goes on your body is as important as what goes in it. The skin is highly porous and contains neuro-transmitters and hormones that are affected by carcinogens. A revolutionary new line of skin care products has been produced ultilizing non-carcinogenic ingredients that have never before been used by the cosmetics industry. For information: VITAL LIFE RESOURCES: #7 Avenida Vista Grande, Suite B-7-163, Santa Fe, NM 87505 (888)-749-3729

FABULOUS HAIR, SKIN & NAILS. This powdered biotin vitamin supplement for men and women, accelerates hair growth and rejuvenates thinning hair, helps end brittle, split ends, dry skin and weak fingernails. It is easy to digest and leaves no unpleasant aftertaste, is 100% vegetarian, contains no excipients, glazes, or non-nutritive substances. A 40gm bottle contains 360mg biotin and lasts 90 days. NICKERSON INTERNATIONAL, LTD. 12 Schubert St. Dept. B, Staten Is., NY 10305 (800)-642-5377

OTHER PRODUCTS:

RELATED BOOKS: DHEA, Unlocking The Secrets Of The Fountain of Youth by Beth M. Ley. The facts on the anti-aging hormone miracle of the 21st Century. *The Potato Antioxidant* by Beth M. Ley. Information on an amazing antioxidant-coenzyme found in potatoes and other foods that can help with Diabetes, Cataracts, HIV, Liver Disease and more. *How To Fight Osteoporosis and Win!* by Beth M. Ley. Find out about calcium, dairy products and calcium supplements and the health of your bones. BL PUBLICATIONS, 21 Dona Tello, Aliso Viejo, CA 92656 (800)-507-2665

EUROPEAN SIX DAY BIO POWER DIET. This program, developed in Switzerland, is based on more than 30 years of scientific research. High quality vegetable and fruit juices are supplemented by special herbal extracts and a detox tea to keep your body properly nourished. It also includes BioStrath tablets, comprised of plasmolyzed yeast in a balanced composition of proteins, vitamins, trace elements and enzymes. BIOPOWER, INC. 19355 Business Center Dr. #2, Northridge CA 91324 (800)-307-7979

TACHYONIZED™ WATER. Proven to be a valuable ingredient for maintaining radiant health, high energy and addressing imbalanced conditions, these drops, taken sublingually breaks the blood-brain barrier and instantly provides life force energy to the body. Tachyonized™ Silica Gel can strengthen skin, hair, bones, nails, ligaments and tendons. Tachyonized™ Fizz-C provides the body with 2 gm. vitamin C and 7 minerals, all Tachyonized™ to magnify and accelerate their effects on the body's absorption and energy utilization. ADVANCED TACHYON TECHNOLOGIES, 435 Tesconi Ci., Santa Rosa, CA 95401 (800)-966-9341.

SPIRULINA SUPERFOOD. Organic Hawaiian Spirulina is an extremely rich source of whole food phytonutrients, B vitamins, protein and GLA. Nutrex, Inc., the Hawaiian grower makes this superfood available in tablets, powder and crystal flake form. Their product is packed in glass with oxygen absorbers for maximum potency. Nutrex Organic Hawaiian Spirulina is the world's only certified organic blue-green algae. NUTREX, INC., 73-4460 Queen Kaahumanu Hwy., Kailua-Kona HI 96740 (800)-395-1353

REJUVENNATION FROM KAYA KALPA, the Indian Science of Longevity. The 21 Day Rejuvenation Program developed by Joseph Kurian, master of Kaya Kalpa, unlocks energy, youthfulness, mental clarity and inner peace with exclusively combined herbal formulas from the sciences of Ayurveda, Dhanurveda and kaya kalpa. The herbs are presented as teas and in cream form to cleanse and open the 107 marmas (energy channels) from the inside out. The kit can be used at home without altering your daily routine. The herbs are organically grown and processed by hand according to traditions thousands of years old. THE KURIAN PROGRAM, INC., PO Box 4217 Orange CA 92613 (800)-330-6999 www.kurian.com

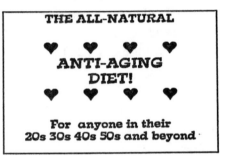

BIBLIOGRAPHY ....

-Abe, S. and Kaneda, T.: **"The effect of edible seaweeds on cholesterol metabolism in rats. In Proceedings of the Seventh International Seaweed Symposium"**, Wiley and Sons, NY, pp. 562-565, 1972

-Aihara, Herman: **Acid & Akaline**, George Oshawa Microbiotic Foundation, 1986

-Albuirmeileh, N. et al**.: "Suppression of Cholesterogenesis by Kyolic and S.-Ally Cysteine"**, The FASEB Jnl, 5:A1756, 1991

-Anderson, J.W.: **"MCF Diet: A Professional Guide"**, 1979

-Anderson, Dr. Richard, ND, NMD: **Cleanse & Purify Thyself,** R. Anderson, 1988

-Aso H.: **"Induction of interferon and activation of NK cells and macrophages in mice by oral administration of Ge-132, an organic germanium compound"**, Microbiol Immunol, 1985, 8(5); 352-353

-Bach, Nelson, USA: **"Finding Balance Through Flower Remedies"**, Healthy & Natural, Vol. 2, No. 1

-Berg, W., Bother, C., and Schneider, H.J.: **"Experimental and Clinical Studies Concerning the Influence of Natural Substances on the Crystallization of Calcium Oxylate"**, Urologe 21:52-58, 1982

-Breuninger, Heather: **"Are Enzymes The Key to Boosting Immunity?"**, Natural Foods Merchandiser, June 1993

-Bricklin, Mark; **Natural Healing**, Rodale Press, 1976

-Bricklin, Mark: **Natural Healing**, Rodale Press, Inc., 1976

-Caporase N., Smith S.M. and Eng R.H.K.: **"Antifungal Activity in Human Urine and Serum After Ingestion of Garlic (Allium sativum)"**, antimicrobial Agents and Chemotherapy, 23: 700-702, 1983

-Chapman, J.B., MD and Perry, Edward L., MD: **The Biochemic Handbook,** Formur, Inc., 1976

-Choi, Steve S.: **"Royal Jelly, the Fountain of Youth"**, Health World, Sept/Oct, 1991

-Cichoke, Anthony J., MA, DC, DACBN: **"Aged Garlic Extract"**, Health & Natural, Vol 2, No.1, 1995

-Cichoke, Anthony J., MA, DC, DACBN: **"Healing Powers of Aged Garlic Extract"**, Townsend Letter for Doctors, June 1994

-Cichoke, Dr. A.J.: **"Enzymes"**, Lets Live, June 1994

-Cichoke, A.J., DC.**:" Systemic Enzyme Therapy"**, The American Chiropractor,April, 1991

-Cichoke, Anthony J.**: "Bee Pollen, The Latest Buzz on the Power of Nectar"**, Body, Mind, Spirit, Feb. - March, 1995

-Cichoke, A.J., DC: **"Fight Back Pain with Enzymes"**, Lets Live, May 1994

-Clark, Linda, M.A.: **"Enzymes can help your health"**, Lets Live, June 1977

-Cutler, Richard, G., PhD: **"Antioxidants and Aging"**, American Journal of Clinical Nutrition, 1991

-**"Daily Vitamin D Can Reduce Fracture Risk"**, Medical Tribune, Aug. 20, 1992

-De Vries, Jan: **Traditional Home & Herbal Remedies,** Mainstream Publishing, 1989

-Dittmar, Mary Jane: **"Getting The Inside Track on Enzymes"**, Health Foods Business, Jan. 1987

-Erasmus, Udo: **"The Value of Fresh Flax Oil"**, Lipid Letter, Issue No.3

-Fallon, Sally W and Enig, Mary G.: **"Soy Products for Dairy Products? Not So Fast.."**, Health Freedom News, Sept, 1995

-Frank, Benjamin S.M.D.: **Nucleic Acid and Anti-Oxidant Therapy of Aging and Degeneration,** Rainstone Publishing, 1977

-Gittleman, Ann Louise; **Super Nutrition for Menopause**, Pocket Books, 1993

-Goldberg, S.L.: **"The Use of Water Soluble Chlorophyll in Oral Sepsis:,** Am. J. Surg 62:117-123, 1943

Goldberg, M.P.D., D.C.: **"Use of Live Enzyme Whole Food in a Chiropractic Practice: One Practicioner's Experience"**, American Chiropracter, July 1990

-Golden T, and Burke, J.F..:**" Effective Management of Offensive Odors."** Gastroenterology 31:260-265, 1956

-Gruskin, G.: **"Chlorophyll -Its Therapeutic Place in Acute and Suppurative Disease"**, Am. J. Surg 49:49-54, 1940

-Heimlich, Jane: **"What Your Doctor Won't Tell You"**, Phillips Publishing, Apr. 1992

-Holly, Cory, DN: **"Your Liver, Your Life"**, Alive Magazine, #137

-Howell, Dr. Edward : **Enzyme Nutrition,** Avery Publishing, 1985

-Hughes, David B., Hoover, Dallas G.: **"Bifidobacteria: Their Potential for Use in American Dairy Products"** Food Technology, April 1991

-Huntoon, Jenefer Scripps, N.D.: **"Consumer Education Series: Enzymes",** Health Foods Business, March 1989

-I-San Lin, Dr. Robert: **Garlic & Health,** International Academy of Health and Fitness, Inc., 1994

-Imada O.: **"Toxicity Aspect of Garlic",** In abstract of the First World Congress on the Health Significance of Garlic and Garlic Constituents, p 47, 1990

-**In Health,** Naturopathic Physician, Vol 2, No.2

-Jarvis, DC: **Folk Medicine,** Fawcett Crest, 1958

-Jensen, Bernard, Ph.D.: **Chlorella, Jewel of the Far East,** Bernard Jensen, 1992

-Jesswith, Sophia: **"Living food",** Alive magazine, #148

-Jones, Susan Smith, Ph.D.: **"Killer Fats vs. Healing Fats"**

-Kamen, Betty, Ph.D.: **"Bee Pollen" From Principles to Practice",** Health Food Business, April 1991

-Kamen, Betty, Ph.D.: **"Avoiding and Reversing Osteoporosis",** Natural Solutions, Vol ii, Issue I, Winter, 1994

-Konishi F, Tanaka K, Himeno K et al: **"Antitumor effect induced by a hot Water extract of Chlorella vulgaris (CE): resistance to Meth-A Tumor Growth Mediated by CE - induced Polymorphonuclear Leukocytes.",** Cancer Immunol Immunother 19:73-78, 1985

-Kotulak, Ronald, Gorner, Peter: **Aging on Hold,** Tribune Publishing, 1992

-Kulawiec, Matthew H.: **"Keep the Colon Clean",** Alive Magazine, #157 Nov. 1995

-Lau, B.H.S., Ong, P., and Tosk, J.:**"Macrohpage chemiluminescence modulated by Chinese medicinal herbs** *Astragalus membranaceus* **and** *Ligustrum lucidum***",** Phytotherapy Res. 3:148-153, 1989

-Lau, Benjamin H.S., MD, PhD: **Garlic Research Update,** Odyssey Publishing, 1991

-Lau, Benjamin H.S.,MD., PhD: **"Detoxifying, Radioprotective and Phagocyte-enhancing effects of Garlic",** International Clinical Nutrition Review, Jan, 1989, Vol 9 No. 1

-Lau, B.H.S., et al.: **"Superiority of Intralesional Immunotherapy with C-Cynebacterium parvum and Allium sativum in Control of Murine Transitional Cell Carcinoma"**, The Jnl. of Urology, 136:701-705, 1986

-Lawson,L.D. and Hughes, B.G.: **" Characterization of Formation of Allicin and Other Thiosulfinates from Garlic"**, Planta Medica 58: 345-350, 1992

-Lee, Lita:, **"Prostate Problems"**, Earthletter, Winter, 1993

-Lee, Lita: Menopause, **Osteoporosis & the ERT Fairy Tale**, Earthletter, Vol 4

No. 2, Summer 1994

-Lee, Lita: **"Anti-tumor properties of natural progesterone"**, Earthletter, Spring, 1993

-Lee, Lita: **"Hypothyroidsm, a modern epidemic?"**, Earthletter, Spring, 1994

-Lee, Lita: **"Cyclic seizures due to estrogen toxicity"**, Earthletter, Summer, 1993

-Lee, LIta: **"Estrogen Mimics: Xenoestrogens"**, Earthletter, Fall, 1994

-Lee, Lita PhD : **Radiation Protection Manual,** Grassroots Network, 1990

-Lewin, Renate:**"Rediscovering Flax: Essential Fats and Fiber in a Single Package"**, Lets' Live, Jan. 1989

-Liu, J. et al.: **"Inhibition of 7,12-dimethylbenz(a)anthracene-induced Mammary Tumors and DNA Adducts by Garlic Powder"**, Carcinogenesis, 13: 1847-1851, 1992

-Loomis, Howard, D.C. and Sutliff, Kris, PhD: **"Improve Digestion with Plant Enzymes"**, The American Chiropractor, Feb. 1990

-Loomis, Howard, D.C.: **"Practical Applications of Enzyme Nutrition: Improve Digestion with Plant Enzymes"**, The American Chiropractor, Feb. 1990

-Lorenzi, G., Cogoli, A.: **"Effect of plasmolysed yeast preparations (BIO-STRATH) on cellular functions"**, Swiss Biotech (6)

-McAuliff, Jill: **"Can Herbs the the answer to the problem of Hair Loss?"**, Healthy and Natural, Vol. 2 No. 2

-Mann, John, Kelly, Aidan A., Ph.D., Dravnieks, Dzintar, Ph.D.: **Secrets of Life Extension,** And/Or Press, 1978

-McClure, Steven, N.D.: **"Raw Power Plus"**, Reflections, Spring, 1988

-Messina, Mark, PhD,Virginia Messina, RD,Setchell, Kenneth, D.R., PhD : **The Simple Soybean and Your Health,** Avery Publishing, 1994

-Mertlew, Gillian, N.D.: **Electrolytes, The Spark of Life,** Nature's Publishing, 1994

-Meyerowitz, Steve: **Wheatgrass, Nature's Finest Medicine,** The Sprout House, Inc., 1991

-Mitsuoka, Tomotari, PhD: **The Secret of Bifidobacteria that Protect our Health",** Tokyo University

-Mitsuoka, Tomotari PhD: **"Intestinal Flora and Aging",** Nutrition Reviews, Vol 50 No. 12

-Murray, Frank : **"Royal Jelly, It's not just for queen bees",** Better Nutrition, August, 1990

-Nakayama S., Yoshisa S., Horao Y, et al.: **"Cytoprotective activity of components of garlic, ginseng, and ciuwijia on hepatocyte injury induced by carbon tetrachloride in vitro:,** Hiroshima J. Med Sci, 1985; 5:460-461

-Negeshi, T. Arimosto, S., Nashizaki, C. et al:: **" Inhibitory Effect of Chlorophyll on the Genotoxicity of 3-amino-1-methyl5H=pyridol (4,3-b)-indole (Try P-2)",** Carcinogenesis 10:145-149, 1989

-Nishino H., Nishino A., Takayasu J. et al.: **"Antitumor-Promoting Activity of Allixin, a Stress Compound Produced by Garlic",** Cancer J. 3"20-21, 1990

-**Nutritional Enzymes: Questions and Answers,** National Enzyme Co., July 1993

-Peat, Ray; **"The Progesterone Deception,"** Townsend Letter for Doctors, Nov., 1987.

-Pierson, Dr. Herbert: **"Synopsis of Designer foods III Phytochemicals in Garlic, Soy & Licorice",** Georgetown University, June 2, 1994

-Quillin, P.: **Healing Nutrients,** Random House, 1987

-Quinn, Dick: **Left For Dead,** Quinn Publishing, 1994

-Qureshi, A.A. et al.: **"Inhibition of Cholesterol Synthesis by Kyolic (Aged Garlic Extract) and S-Allyl Cysteine in a Hypercholesterolemic Model",** Abstracts of the FirstWorld

Congress on the Health Significance of Garlic and Garlic Constituents, pp17, 1990

-Ratcliff, J.D.: **"Enzymes, Medicine's Bright Hope"**, The Reader's Digest, June 1961

-Rector-Page, Linda, ND, PhD: **Detoxification & Body Cleansing,** Healthy Healing Publications, 1993

-Rochefort, Henri: **"Do Anti-Estrogens and Anti-progestins act as Hormone-antagonists or recepter targeted drugs in Breast Cancer?",** Trends in Pharmaceutical Sciences, April 1987

-Roderick, Dave: **"Skin Therapy and Osteoporosis",** Clinical Nutrition News, 1995

-Rogers, Sherry, M.D.: **"Enzymes fight cancer",** Lets Live, May 1995

-Rothschild, P.R., Ordoniz, L.,: **"Absorption Study with SOC/CAT®",** Univ. Labs Press

-St. Claire, Debra: **"American and European Herbology",** Healthy & Natural, Vol. 2, No. 1

-Schecter, Steven R.: **"Welcome to the Pollen Nation",** Healthy & Natural Vol.2 Issue 3

-Schwontkowski, Dr. Donna: **"Herbal Treasures of the Rainforest",** Healthy & Natural , Oct. 1994

-Sheer, James F.: **"Dethrone aging with Royal Jelly",** Better Nutrition, June, 1995

-Seibold, Ronald L., M.S.: **Cereal Grass What's In It For You!,** Wilderness Community Education Foundation, Inc., 1990

-SGP---**"The therapeutic Garlic**. Osaka, The Wakunaga Pharmaceutical Company, 1987

-SGP---**Wakunaga Probiotics For Maintaining a Healthy Intestinal Flora for Normal Digestive Function,** The Wakunaga Pharmaceutical Corp., 1995

-Spake, Amanda: **"Maverick Scientist Devra Lee Davis is Afraid She Knows the Answer",** Health, October, 1995

-Spectrum Naturals: **"Basic Facts on Fats and Oils,"** Spectrum, 1993

-Spectrum Naturals: **"Organic Flax Seed Oil",** Spectrum, 1993

-Strause, Linda, Saltman, Paul et al.: **"Spinal Bone Loss in Postmenopausal Women Supplemented with Calcium and Trace Minerals",** Jnl. of Nutrition, 1994 p 1060-1064

-Sumiyoshi, H. and Wargovich, M.J.: **"Chemoprevention of 1,2-dimethylhydrazine-induced Colon Cancer in Mice by Naturally Occurring Organosulfur Compounds"**, Cancer Res., 50:5084-5087, 1990

-Suzuki, F, Pollard RB: **"Prevention of suppressed gamma-interferon production in thermally injured mice by administration of novel organogermanium compound Ge-132"**, J. Interferon Res, 1984; 4:223-233

-Tadi, Padama P.M.S., Teel, Robert W., PhD., and Lau, Benjamin, H.S., MD, PhD: **"Anticandidal and Anticarcinogenic Potentials of Garlic"**, Integrated Therapies, 1990

-Takeyama, H. et al.: **"Growth Inhibition and Modulation of Cell Markers of Melanoma by S-allyCysteine"**, Oncology, 50:63-39, 1993

-Tanaka K, Konishi F, Mimeno K et al: **"Augmentation of antitumor resistance by a strain of unicellular green algae, Chlorella vulgaris,"** Cancer Immunol Immunother 17:90-94, 1984

-Teas J.: **"The consumption of seaweed as a protective factor in the etiology of breast cancer"**, Med. Hypotheses 7:601-613, 1981

-Teas, J.: **"The dietary intake of Laminaria, a brown seaweed and breast cancer prevention"**, Nutr. Cancer 4:217-222, 1983

-Terwel, L. and Van der Hoeven, J.C.M.: **"Antimutagenic Activity of Some Naturally Occurring Compounds Towards Cigarette-smoke Condensate and Benzoalpyrene in the Salmonella/microsome Assay"**, Mutation Res 152:1-4, 1985

-Tho, L.L. and Candlish, J.K.:**"Superoxide Dismutase and Glutathione Peroxidase Activities in Erythrocytes as Indices of Oxygen Loading Disease: A Survey of 100 cases."**, Biochemical Medicine and Metabolic Biology, 38, 365-373, 1987

-Thomas, John: **Young Again! How to Reverse the Aging Process,** Plexus Press, 1994

-Tobe, John : **"Enzymes: Nature's Metabolizers"**, Cancer Forum, Summer 1995

-Tosk, J., Lau, B.H.S., Jui, Pl, Myers, R.C. and Torrey, R.R.: **"Chemiluminescence in a macrophage cell line modulated by biological response modifiers."**, J.Leukocyte Biol. 46:103-108, 1989

-Vogel, A. MD: **Book of Fourteen Amazing Herbal Medicines,** Keats Publishing, 1990

-Yamagishi, Yoshio, Yaguchi, Isamu, Kenmoku, Yukie: **"Clinical Studies on Chlorella"**, "Nippon Iji Shimpo", 17-18 (No. 2196), May 28, 1966

-Yu t-H and Wuc-m: **"Stability of Allicin in Garlic Juice"**, J. Food Sci. 54: 977-981, 1989

-Yeh, Y.Y., et al.: **"Hypolipidemic Effects of Garlic Extract in Vivo and in Vitro"**, Absteracts of the First World Congress on the Health Significance ofGarlic and Garlic Constituents, pp.37, 1990

-Ziegler, Jan: **"Just the Flax, Ma'am: Researchers Testing Linseed,"** Journal of the National Cancer Inst. 86(23):1746-1748, Dec. 7, 1994

—A—

acid/alkaline, 21
Acidophilus, 27, 28, 133, 135
acne, 88, 91, 92, 101, 142
adrenal, 98, 99, 100, 101
adrenals, 20, 100, 108, 119
AFB, 80
AGE, 77, 78, 81, 109, 124, 134
age spots, 48, 84, 92
Aged Garlic Extract, 22, 73, 75, 78, 79, 133
aging, 1, 2, 5, 7, 19, 20, 27, 33, 37, 41, 48, 49, 51, 55, 61, 63, 65, 69, 75, 77, 79, 83, 84, 86, 87, 89, 102, 103, 109, 115, 135, 138, 142
AHA, 84, 141
AIDS, 74, 77, 79
Albert Schweitzer, 74
alcohol, 21, 23, 27, 98, 106, 109, 138
alfalfa, 137
algae, 66, 68, 69, 84, 87, 91
alkalize, 22, 63
allergies, 4, 41, 44, 48, 67, 83, 120, 121, 135
allicin, 76
allopathic, 26
aloe, 23, 88, 110, 141
aluminum, 32, 38
Alzheimer's, 38, 77
amino acids, 1, 3, 29, 38, 40, 43, 65, 68, 75, 85, 107, 140
anemia, 25, 39
antibiotics, 27, 107
antibodies, 65
antifungal, 58, 74
antioxidants, 2, 8, 41, 63, 89, 93, 137
aosain, 84
arteries, 7, 39, 49, 50, 55, 78, 139
arteriosclerosis, 78
artery, 39, 55, 79, 139
arthritis, 36, 49, 50, 57, 64, 73, 79, 103, 110, 111, 120, 139, 140
Aspergillus, 80
asthma, 49, 57, 67, 105, 107
athlete, 39, 40, 51, 73, 87

—B—

babies, 44, 50, 55
back pain, 41, 110, 136

bacteria, 4, 19, 21, 24, 27, 28, 29, 33, 45, 58, 62, 63, 83, 84, 86, 107, 133, 134
baldness, 67, 103
barley, 45, 62, 63, 64, 65, 70, 96, 134, 136, 137
bentonite, 25
BHA, 84
Bifidobacterium, 27, 28
bioavailable, 28, 45, 134, 135
bioflavonoids, 65
blindness, 25
blood, 1, 2, 4, 5, 6, 7, 19, 20, 22, 24, 25, 38, 39, 41, 44, 46, 50, 51, 54, 55, 56, 58, 62, 63, 67, 69, 70, 74, 75, 77, 78, 79, 93, 95, 96, 97, 98, 99, 102, 103, 104, 109, 111, 117, 119
blood thinner, 79, 99
bone, 20, 57, 95, 96, 97, 98, 99, 103, 107, 123, 125, 126
Borage, 103, 138
bowel, 4, 7, 24, 57
brains, 6, 38
brittle nails, 57

—C—

caffeine, 23, 83, 101, 109
Calc. Fluor., 93, 110, 113
calcium, 20, 31, 33, 34, 38, 39, 46, 62, 63, 64, 67, 75, 92, 93, 95, 96, 97, 98, 110, 113, 136
cancer, 22, 24, 28, 46, 47, 48, 50, 53, 54, 55, 56, 58, 62, 63, 64, 68, 69, 73, 75, 76, 77, 79, 80, 83, 99, 101, 105, 106, 107, 118
Candida, 33, 45, 78
capillaries, 7, 38, 102, 106
carbohydrates, 1, 3, 23, 29, 43, 134
carcinogen, 77, 80
Cascara Sagrada, 26
Catalase, 47, 48, 77
cell, 2, 6, 7, 8, 20, 33, 45, 47, 49, 53, 56, 68, 69, 74, 79, 83, 85, 86, 88, 92, 93, 104, 106, 110, 113, 135, 141
cellulase, 42, 43, 138
cellulite, 87, 90
cereal grass, 21, 23, 63, 64, 65, 66, 70, 108
chelating, 33
chemical sensitivity, 23

chew, 2, 111
Chlorella, 23, 62, 63, 66, 68, 69, 70, 71
chlorophyll, 22, 54, 63, 64, 65, 68, 70,
   137, 138
cholesterol, 23, 49, 54, 58, 62, 67, 69,
   73, 77, 78, 79, 99, 101
chromium, 32, 39
circulation, 5, 7, 38, 62, 78, 90, 91, 92,
   93, 99, 105
clogged pores, 87
clot, 57, 77, 79
coffee, 7, 21, 98, 99
colitis, 24
collagen, 47, 83, 85, 93
Colloidal, 38
constipation, 21, 23, 24, 73, 101
copper, 32, 33, 39, 54, 75, 97
corn, 4, 53, 54, 80
cough, 140
cross linking, 48
Crystalloid, 37, 86, 89

—D—

dairy, 21, 23, 35, 46, 64, 96, 134
dark circles, 90, 91
degenerative disease, 19, 21, 42, 45, 55,
   61, 79
dehydration, 84, 85
depression, 23, 57, 77, 96, 100, 101,
   112, 119, 139
detoxify, 41, 48
diabetes, 41, 49, 55, 58, 123
diarrhea, 21, 26, 74, 105
digestion, 2, 23, 41, 42, 43, 45, 46, 50,
   51, 68, 83, 98
digestive enzymes, 28, 41, 42, 45, 51
digestive tract, 19, 24, 25, 51, 58, 93,
   134
diverticulitis, 24
dizziness, 23
DNA, 55, 64, 68, 77, 80, 106
Dong Quai, 111
Dr. Benjamin Lau, 62
Dr. Edward Howell, 42
Dr. John Milner, 77
Dr. Manfred Steins, 78
Dr. Sherry Rogers, 50
Dr. Tariq Abdullah, 74
Dr. Walter Willet, 55
dry skin, 57, 86, 88, 142

—E—

Echinacea, 22, 45, 112
EFA, 56, 57, 138
EFAs, 57, 58, 138
elastase, 83, 85
elastin, 83, 85, 93
elderly, 50, 62, 116
electrolytes, 6, 22, 32, 37, 39, 40, 47,
   85, 86, 90, 91, 96, 136, 139
elimination, 2, 7, 23, 25, 26, 83
emotional problems, 119
endocrine, 101, 102
enzyme inhibitors, 46, 47
Enzymes, 2, 3, 4, 6, 7, 23, 27, 28, 29,
   33, 36, 37, 39, 41, 42, 43, 44, 45,
   46, 47, 48, 49, 50, 51, 63, 65, 70,
   77, 80, 87, 98, 99, 101, 107, 134,
   137, 138, 139, 142
epidermis, 85
Epsom salts, 26, 111
essential fatty acids, 43, 53, 56, 136
estrogen, 20, 58, 84, 97, 98, 99, 100,
   101
Evening Primrose Oil, 138
exercise, 5, 51, 58, 82, 90, 104, 123,
   124, 125, 126, 127, 128, 129, 132
exfoliation, 84
eyes, 6, 27, 44, 51, 91

—F—

fast, 6, 22, 125
fatigue, 4, 23, 39, 77, 96, 100, 133
fats, 1, 3, 23, 39, 43, 49, 50, 53, 54, 55,
   58, 83, 102, 134
fatty acids, 3, 43, 53, 54, 56, 57, 58,
   100, 136, 138
Fennel, 26
fermented soy, 46
fiber, 4, 5, 43, 58, 82, 83, 136
flax, 50, 54, 57, 58, 100, 136, 138
flower, 23, 106, 108, 140
food allergies, 44, 83
foremen, 57
free radical scavengers, 37
free radicals, 7, 40, 47, 48, 64, 92, 137

—G—

garlic, 23, 29, 53, 73, 74, 75, 76, 77,
   78, 79, 80, 81, 82, 113, 133

gastrointestinal, 42, 43, 67
genetic, 4, 68, 83, 102
germanium, 75
ginger, 71
ginseng, 5, 112
GLA, 58, 99, 103, 137
glucose, 3, 4
Golden Seal, 26, 112
Gotu kola, 22
grain, 4, 5, 45, 64
gray hair, 67
green papaya, 49, 87, 89, 93, 137, 141
growth depressants, 46

—H—

hair, 1, 6, 27, 46, 51, 57, 67, 81, 87, 89,
    101, 102, 110, 135, 141
hair loss, 57, 102
headaches, 22, 25, 26, 100, 140
healing crisis, 51
heart, 6, 39, 48, 50, 53, 54, 55, 56, 57,
    58, 73, 77, 78, 79, 96, 100, 105,
    115, 123
heart disease, 48, 53, 54, 55, 56, 57, 58,
    77, 78, 123
heart palpitations, 96
heavy metal, 22, 73, 76, 135
herbs, 22, 23, 25, 26, 86, 90, 91, 100,
    105, 106, 108, 112, 133, 134, 135,
    137, 139, 141
homeopathic, 90, 92, 93, 106, 108, 110,
    111, 134, 140, 142
homeostasis, 32, 37, 96, 135
homogenized, 6
honey, 35, 88, 107, 141
hormones, 20, 23, 59, 65, 78, 96, 97,
    100, 101, 104, 107, 139
hot flashes, 95, 98, 99, 100, 111, 133
Hunza's, 31
hydrochloric acid, 41, 49
hydrogenated, 54, 55, 56, 102, 103

—I—

immune system, 4, 19, 24, 25, 27, 33,
    36, 44, 48, 57, 58, 62, 68, 74, 75,
    77, 78, 80, 81, 87, 102, 103, 107,
    117, 119, 120, 122, 135
inflammation, 41, 42, 103, 105, 112,
    139
influenza, 27, 78

intestinal flora, 7, 27, 81
intestine, 3, 4, 27, 28, 43
iodine, 32, 67
iron, 7, 32, 39, 46, 62, 65, 75, 92, 96
irritability, 97

—J—

joints, 36, 40, 103, 104, 110
jojoba, 89, 90, 92

—K—

kale, 96
kelp, 68, 70, 87, 89, 91, 108, 110, 134,
    135
kidney, 21, 25, 55, 63, 91, 107
kidney stones, 63
Kyolic, 73, 74, 75, 76, 77, 78, 79, 81,
    82, 134

—L—

L.O. Pilgeram, 50
LDL, 55, 78, 79
leaky gut, 27, 44, 55
lecithin, 54, 106, 136
ligaments, 40, 126
lignin, 58
linoleic, 57, 58
linolenic, 57, 99
lipase, 42, 43, 47, 49, 50, 134, 138
Lita Lee, 44
liver, 6, 8, 22, 23, 24, 25, 26, 50, 51,
    55, 58, 76, 77, 80, 83, 84, 86, 89,
    91, 93, 100, 107, 111, 119
Lobelia, 26
loofah, 92
lumbar, 41
lungs, 1, 6, 123
lymph glands, 22
lymphatic, 44
lymphocytes, 29, 80

—M—

macrophages, 27, 62
Mag. Phos., 110, 112
magnesium, 33, 34, 38, 39, 46, 63, 67,
    75, 87, 89, 92, 93, 96, 97, 98, 110,
    113, 136
maldigestion, 5, 7

malnutrition, 24
manganese, 33, 39, 97
margarine, 6, 55, 102
meat, 21, 36, 39, 46, 64, 111
membranes, 2, 26, 28, 75, 83, 104
menopausal, 83, 97, 99, 100, 101, 123
mercury, 48, 75
metabolic, 6, 33, 34, 39, 42, 45, 51, 126
metabolic enzymes, 6, 42, 45, 51
metabolism, 1, 5, 20, 27, 36, 40, 50, 53, 55, 57, 63, 67, 80, 97, 98, 139
Methionine Reductase, 48
micronutrient, 66, 67, 135
migraines, 57
minerals, 2, 3, 4, 6, 22, 23, 29, 31, 32, 33, 34, 36, 37, 38, 39, 40, 42, 46, 47, 54, 57, 61, 63, 67, 68, 70, 75, 85, 89, 91, 92, 93, 96, 97, 103, 107, 126, 134, 135, 136, 137, 138, 139, 141, 142
morning sickness, 45
mucoid, 24, 25, 26
muscle, 25, 39, 48, 59, 90, 123, 125, 126, 127, 132, 136
Muscular Dystrophy, 49
mutation, 63, 64
myofibrosis, 36
Myrrh, 25

—N—

NaPCA, 85, 88, 91, 92
Nat. Mur., 92, 110
Nat. Phos., 112
Nat. Sulph., 112
natural progesterone, 98, 99, 101
naturopathic, 26, 99
nausea, 22
neurotransmitters, 65
nose, 44
nutrients, 2, 3, 5, 7, 19, 27, 32, 40, 43, 45, 46, 50, 54, 56, 57, 61, 62, 64, 67, 70, 75, 86, 87, 89, 97, 102, 106, 135, 136, 138, 139, 141
nutritional yeast, 103, 110, 134

—O—

oils, 35, 54, 55, 56, 57, 58, 86, 87, 89, 90, 91, 92, 100, 103, 133, 138
olive oil, 23, 26, 56

organs, 5, 19, 20, 21, 22, 36, 51, 55, 69, 117, 119
osteoporosis, 95, 98, 99, 123, 136
ovaries, 101
oxygen, 1, 7, 8, 22, 36, 37, 38, 39, 48, 76, 86, 89, 90, 91, 92, 93, 100, 102, 139

—P—

pancreas, 26, 45, 46, 47
parasites, 19, 24, 25, 55
pasteurized, 6
penile, 39
pepsin, 42, 43
peptides, 101
Peroxidation, 75
petroleum, 87, 89, 91, 100
pH, 21, 22, 27, 31, 33, 34, 36, 43, 51, 63, 65, 84, 88, 92, 95, 135, 141, 143
phosphorus, 20, 33
phytates, 46
phytosterols, 101
pituitary, 100
plant enzymes, 3, 42, 43, 51, 98, 137
platelets, 79
PMS, 23, 58, 67, 83, 139
poison, 5, 19
pollution, 19, 36, 44, 48, 75, 86
poor circulation, 7
postmenopausal, 99
potassium, 20, 34, 63, 67, 75, 97
potatoes, 21, 35, 80, 109
premature aging, 51, 75, 79, 142
progesterone, 20, 98, 99, 100, 101, 102
prostaglandin, 55
protease, 42, 43, 45, 46, 98, 134, 138
protein, 1, 29, 33, 36, 38, 42, 43, 46, 47, 50, 62, 64, 65, 68, 85, 86, 137
psyllium, 25
puffy eyes, 91

—R—

rheumatoid arthritis, 50, 103, 120
Rhubarb, 26
royal jelly, 23, 95, 103, 106, 113

—S—

S.O.D., 47, 48, 135
SAC, 77

saliva, 2, 3
sea vegetables, 66, 70, 108
selenium, 32, 48, 62, 75, 89
shark liver oil, 86
shaving, 88
silica, 22, 86, 89, 90, 113
skin, 6, 19, 20, 23, 25, 27, 37, 41, 44,
   47, 48, 49, 51, 57, 58, 67, 75, 80,
   83, 84, 85, 86, 87, 88, 89, 90, 91,
   92, 93, 98, 107, 109, 115, 133, 141,
   142, 143
small intestine, 3, 27, 28, 43
soy, 46, 102
sperm, 20, 39, 41, 112
sprouts, 21
squalane, 86, 90, 91, 93
stamina, 39, 70, 133
starch, 2, 4, 47
starch blockers, 47
steroids, 33, 119
stomach, 2, 3, 25, 26, 28, 33, 43, 49,
   64, 73, 77, 107, 109
stress, 1, 27, 51, 67, 75, 77, 80, 81, 83,
   84, 89, 96, 98, 104, 108, 119, 126,
   132, 133, 140
sugar, 7, 20, 36, 39, 56, 58, 83, 84, 96,
   97, 101, 107
sunflower, 45, 89, 92, 141
supplements, 5, 6, 27, 28, 32, 38, 41,
   61, 64, 65, 70, 76, 77, 80, 107, 108,
   111, 113, 133, 134, 135, 137, 138

—T—

tendons, 40, 126
throat, 73, 81
thymus, 107
thyroid, 20, 67, 99, 100, 101
toxin, 27, 80, 92
trace minerals, 6, 32, 38, 39, 40, 54, 85,
   89, 91, 92, 93, 97, 135
tremors, 50, 97

trypsin, 42, 45, 46

ulcer, 62, 82

vertebra, 41
vetebra, 41
virus, 47, 58, 81
vitamin B12, 38
vitamin C, 6, 33, 65, 68, 99
vitamin D, 33, 97
vitamins, 2, 3, 4, 23, 24, 28, 29, 33, 36,
   42, 47, 57, 61, 62, 65, 68, 70, 75,
   107, 133, 135, 136, 137, 138, 139,
   140, 142
vomiting, 21

—W—

waste, 2, 4, 5, 6, 7, 25, 26, 34, 57, 103,
   133
water retention, 87, 100
wheat grass, 61, 62, 63, 70, 134
white blood cells, 44, 117
wild yam, 99, 101, 138
worms, 24
wrinkle, 1, 51, 58, 86
wrinkles, 27, 41, 48, 58, 83, 84, 88, 93,
   142

—Y—

yeast, 4, 28, 29, 33, 45, 103, 110, 133,
   134

—Z—

Zinc, 39, 47, 57, 62, 66